Splendid
NEEDLEPOINT

Splendid
NEEDLEPOINT

40 Beautiful & Distinctive Designs

CATHERINE REURS

Lark
Books

Asheville, North Carolina

EDITOR: **Deborah Morgenthal**
ART DIRECTOR: **Chris Bryant**
PRODUCTION: **Chris Bryant, Bobby Gold**

Library of Congress Cataloging-in-Publication Data

Reurs, Catherine.
   Splendid needlepoint : 40 beautiful & distinctive designs /
   Catherine Reurs
      p.   cm.
   Includes index.
   ISBN 1-887374-22-1
   1. Canvas embroidery—Patterns.   I. Title
   TT778.C3R445   1997
   746.44'2041—dc20   96-38274
                                                CIP

10 9 8 7 6 5 4 3

Published in 1996 by Lark Books
50 College Street
Asheville, NC 28801
USA

Distributed by Random House,Inc., in the United States, Canada, the United Kingdom, Europe, and Asia

Distributed in Australia by Capricorn Link (Australia) Pty Ltd.,
P.O. Box 6651, Baulkham Hills Business Centre, NSW 2153, Australia

Distributed in New Zealand by Tandem Press Ltd.,
2 Rugby Rd., Birkenhead, Auckland, New Zealand

Printed in Hong Kong

ISBN 1-887374-22-1

Contents

INTRODUCTION

EVER SINCE I WAS A YOUNG GIRL, I HAVE LOVED PLAYING WITH COLOR, PATTERN, AND TEXTILES. I sewed, crocheted, painted, wove baskets, and made beaded pieces. During my teenage years, my local wool shop began to carry needlepoint canvases. The designs did not appeal to me but I was attracted by the medium. The shop owner very kindly offered to sell me blank canvas, and cautioned me to start on something small and not too complex. Using a book, I taught myself the basic stitch and, completely ignoring the shop owner's advice, designed a 22-inch pillow on 14-mesh canvas that was inspired by three intricate oriental carpets! Of course, the pillow took me more than three years to finish, but I created something that I really loved and I had found the medium for my creative wandering. I love everything about needlepoint—the freedom to stitch how and where I want...the interplay of color upon color and texture upon texture...the freedom to modify a design along the way.

To me, needlepoint is an incredibly liberating textile medium because you can start anywhere on the canvas and stitch whatever you want to. You don't have to start at the bottom and work your way up or vice versa. When you feel like concentrating you can stitch the design areas, a task that requires attention to detail; when you want to relax you can stitch the back-

ground, a soothing and repetitive job. Needlepoint is very portable, and I love the fact that I can do it pretty much anywhere. It takes time—there is no getting around that fact—but once the needlepoint is completed, it will give you years and years of unending pleasure.

Many people ask me where I find the inspiration for my work. The answer is—everywhere. Ideas come from everywhere... inspiration is everywhere: you just have to open yourself so that you can "see" ideas and focus on them. When I see something that I love, that speaks to me, I use it as the basis of a design. It's that simple. I tend to find inspiration in things I love that are very close at hand—my cats, old textiles, flowers in the garden, magazines, books, museums, even television shows and films. I carry a tiny spiral-bound notebook in which I constantly make notes ("do cat in a bucket with forsythia background") and quickly draw horrible little thumbnail sketches for my use only. These sketches are definitely not works of art! But they serve to remind me of the idea I had. Ideas come in a flash and in strange places (in bed, on airplanes, in the shower, during a walk, while shopping), and I learned a long time ago that if you don't capture them on paper right away they are nearly impossible to reconstruct.

As my family and friends are happy to point out, I like to collect things...too many things...and I have very eclectic taste—new

and antique textiles, cobalt glass, lace, beads, Santas and Christmas ornaments, blue and white china, shells, glass paintings, and anything with cherubs and cats. Books and magazines are the most important part of my collection: my studio floor groans from the weight of hundreds of them. I clip images and articles from magazines and file them by subject; my books are organized by subject. I keep them carefully organized because they are valuable resources, and I constantly refer to them as starting points for creating designs.

The drawback of a love affair with needlework is that there are never enough hours in the day to accomplish all you want to. I have so many sketchbooks filled with ideas that I'd probably have to live a hundred lifetimes to bring to life all the designs waiting inside them. The good news is that I have lots of ideas to choose from!

In this, my second book, I've begun the exciting process of experimenting with new fibers, and it has opened a whole new world of possibilities. I greatly appreciate all the letters and suggestions I've received from readers of *In Splendid Detail*. The most frequent request was that every design be charted—in this book they all are. Also, wherever possible, I have listed mail-order suppliers for all the products I have used in these designs.

For this book I wanted to include a broad spectrum of design subjects that can be stitched with a variety of fibers, and to offer a wide range of project sizes, from a small pincushion to a full-sized pillow. I know many of you are generous stitchers who like to make needlepoint gifts; for you I have included more small- and medium-sized projects. These also work well for those of you with very little "free" time who want to stitch something beautiful (smaller projects equal faster gratification!). I hope you will enjoy these new designs. I encourage you to personalize them to suit your needs and desires.

MEDIEVAL FOX PILLOW, PAGE 29

FACING PAGE, TOP RIGHT, BY DROPPING IN HALLOWEEN COLORS FOR THE BACKGROUND, THE "SOCKS" CAT (PAGE 40) SUDDENLY BECOMES A HALLOWEEN CAT.

H ERE ARE A FEW TECHNIQUES THAT
YOU CAN EXPERIMENT WITH, and
ways that you can alter my needlepoint
designs to give them your personal touch.

COLOR

I have intentionally stitched several of the
designs in the book in a variety of "color-
ways." You can see in my cat designs
(page 38) that by dropping in Halloween
colors for the background the "socks" cat
suddenly becomes a Halloween cat. The
gray tabby cat looks sedate against a green
background but really jumps out against a
pink background.

Other good examples of color substitu-
tion are my cherry and lemon designs on
page 65. The cherries and lemons with
their checkerboard borders are all stitched
using exactly the same colors. What I have
varied are the background colors, and, as a
result, the same fruits look dramatically different from piece to piece. This happens
because all colors "reflect" the colors that
are near them (white next to yellow takes
on a yellow tinge, red next to blue takes on
a blue cast, etc.).

Color variations can also completely
change the way we perceive a pattern. The
miniature Amish quilt pieces on page 72
look like nine different patterns, but they
are actually only two patterns. They were
stitched in nine color combinations which
makes each one look completely different
from the rest. When you stitch, be brave, be
playful, and consider changing the background color of a design so that it perfectly
complements your own decor.

SIZE

If you see a design you like but the size isn't
what you had in mind, try stitching it on a
larger mesh (to enlarge it) or a finer mesh
(to reduce it). In Needlepoint Basics on page
14, I explain how to calculate what the
dimensions of a design will be if you change
the mesh. This is an easy and fun way to
alter a design.

FIBERS

Recently I have begun to use fibers other
than Persian wool. I still love the traditional
look of a needlepoint piece all done in wool,
and wool wears extremely well. However, an
incredible range of new fibers is now available that offers infinite opportunities.

Each type of fiber has a special quality
that can add much interest and liveliness to
your needlework. For a matte texture, try
wool; for a softly reflective texture, try matte
silk, cotton floss, and overdyed cottons; for
furry or fuzzy textures, try angora, mohair,
alpaca, and synthetic suede; for shiny textures, try silk, pearl cotton, and even patent
leather; and for sparkle, give all the metallic
fibers a try.

A judicious use of a contrasting fiber can
change the whole way a textile "reads." By
using a shiny fiber in a matte wool design
you will draw the eye to the shiny areas first,
and, in this way, control how the viewer
reads your needlepoint. You can also use
fibers to mimic textures of animal fur or skin:
For my Noah's Ark design on page 18, try
using shiny pearl cotton for the snakes,
frogs, and turtles' shells, fuzzy mohair for the
bunnies' tails, matte silk for the elephants,
tweedy wool for the bears, and softly reflective cotton floss for the penguins.

Metallic fibers can add subtle texture
when used in small amounts, and look very
festive and glitzy when used in large areas.
Try using all metallics and you can turn a
small design into a holiday ornament. It all
depends on what mood or effect you wish to
create. By using different fibers you have the
means to greatly increase the vocabulary and
power of expression in your needlepoint.

FINISHING

Well-designed and executed finishing is
really important because it acts like a frame
for your needlework. It should complement
and bring out the design without over-
whelming it. If you have access to a well-
stocked home-decorating shop, take your
finished needlepoint piece there and keep
an open mind regarding trims—consider
using brushed fringe or tasselled trim for
your edging, as well as the usual braid or
twisted cording. There are books that can
show you how to make your own twisted
cord; if you have the patience, you can
make cording with fibers that perfectly
complement your needlework. When you
approach finishing in this way, you will not
be at the mercy of what happens to be in
stock at the store.

Years ago I did my own finishing...that
was before I had a pillow professionally finished. I immediately realized that my finisher did a far better job than I did; an
added bonus was the thrill of sending off a
trapezoid, lumpy piece of needlework and
then, some weeks later, receiving a perfectly
finished piece! In this book, I have listed
sources where you can buy the same items
that I used for finishing nonpillow needlepoint pieces, i.e. boxes, pincushions, stool
bases, etc., and I also give the address of
my finisher in case you want to treat yourself—and fine finishing is a treat!

Textiles are my greatest passion, and I
have tried, with these projects, to share that
passion with you. I hope you will enjoy
many, many happy hours stitching designs
from this book. It gives me tremendous sat-
isfaction to think of beginner and experi-
enced stitchers all over the world, in city
and country settings, taking pleasure in
working my designs. I owe you a debt of
gratitude for making it possible for me to
turn my needlepoint avocation into a voca-
tion. When you stitch, I hope you will feel
the same love and excitement I felt when I
created these designs for you.

THE COLOR SCHEME DETERMINES WHAT PART
OF A DESIGN STANDS OUT. *LEFT*, LEMON MAGNETS,
PAGE 65. *RIGHT*, AMISH STAR PATTERN, PAGE 73.

NEEDLEPOINT BASICS

AFTER YEARS OF STITCHING I HAVE FOUND METHODS AND MATERIALS TO SUIT MY PERSONAL WAY OF STITCHING. As you stitch, you will discover your own preferences. Please remember that there are no rules and there is no right or wrong way to do needlepoint. I cannot stress this enough: *there really are no rules and there are no needlepoint police!* You should stitch in the most comfortable and relaxing way for you. If you are a beginner, try small and simple projects, and don't drive yourself crazy by being a perfectionist. You will make mistakes, but needlepoint is a very forgiving medium, and you can pick out the mistakes or stitch over them.

You will learn something from every project you stitch, so the more you stitch the more you'll learn. As your expertise grows, you can, with confidence, aspire to more advanced projects.

In this section I have brought together some basic information about materials, tools, and techniques that I hope will help you with your needlepoint. If you haven't done so before, try doing needlepoint in a variety of ways—on a frame and without a frame, on large-mesh canvas and on fine-mesh canvas, with wool and with other fibers; pretty soon you will know what you like, and which way is most relaxing and rewarding for you.

MATERIALS

CANVAS

Needlepoint is stitched on a special fabric called needlepoint canvas. It is generally made of cotton threads woven together with spaces between the threads. This canvas is treated with a sizing agent to add strength, stiffness, and smoothness which makes stitching easier. Each point where the vertical and horizontal threads of the canvas intersect is stitched so that the entire needlepoint canvas is covered with wool (or other fibers) to create a pleasing design and a completely filled textile surface.

The number of threads to the inch (cm) is called the *gauge* or *mesh count*. If a canvas has ten threads to one inch (2.5 cm), the gauge is called *10 to the inch* (cm) or *10-mesh* or *10-count* (the points where canvas threads cross or intersect are called *meshes*). The higher the number of threads per inch (2.5 cm), the closer together the threads of the canvas will be, and therefore the smaller the stitches will become. Commonly available canvas ranges from 5-mesh (used for rugs) to 24-mesh (used for miniature work such as dollhouse rugs).

Some canvas is available in different colors so that you can match the canvas color to the predominant background color of your design. This is useful because if any canvas shows through it will not be obvious. As my eyes get older I prefer to stitch all my designs on white canvas because it is easier to see. When my design is stitched, I just hold my canvas up to the light to see if there are any stitches I've missed!

Buy the best quality canvas possible; to ensure better wear, buy enough canvas to allow the selvage to run vertically on either side of the design you have chosen. Also, be sure to allow for at least a 3-inch (6 cm) unstitched border of canvas around your entire design. This is very important for blocking the canvas, and also allows you space to stitch some extra rows if you need to.

There are three different types of needlepoint canvas.

INTERLOCK CANVAS

Zweigart Interlock canvas is my personal favorite. The threads that make up interlock canvas are twisted so that they actually lock at each intersection, which prevents the canvas threads from shifting with the tension of the stitches or from fraying around the edges—thus the name interlock. Because interlock canvas is so firmly woven, it is less likely to be pulled out of shape by the stitches. Also, the holes in the canvas are clearly visible, making it a very easy canvas to work on, no matter what your experience level is. Moreover, interlock canvas can be used for any needlepoint stitch.

MONO CANVAS

Also called single-thread canvas, mono canvas is made of single threads woven vertically and horizontally over each other. Mono canvas is a heavy canvas that has lots of "give" and wears well. However, it has a number of drawbacks: (1) Because of its single-thread construction, it tends to unravel more easily than other types of canvas; (2) Because the threads are loosely woven, they tend to slip if you use the *sewing method* (see Stitching Methods on page 12); (3) Mono canvas is considerably more expensive than interlock canvas (generally, most hand-painted canvases are done on mono canvas.); (4) Lastly, you cannot use the half-cross stitch on mono canvas, but only the continental or basketweave stitches.

PENELOPE CANVAS

This canvas is also called double-thread or double-mesh, and is made of double threads that run vertically and horizontally. The advantage to Penelope canvas is that different size stitches can be worked on the same canvas (12-gauge with 24-gauge, for example). You achieve this by skipping a thread, i.e. stitching over two threads for the 12-gauge stitches, and then stitching over every thread for the 24-gauge stitches. This is useful if you have some design areas where you want a lot of detail and other areas where you don't need the detail and can use larger stitches. However, because of the double threads, it can be confusing and difficult to find the correct space into which to insert the needle. And because Penelope canvas is not as easily counted as interlock or mono canvas, it is not well suited for use with charted designs. This canvas should be used for designs requiring two gauges of stitches, and it should always be blocked by a professional because it can be tricky to block.

PLASTIC CANVAS

Not surprisingly, this canvas is made from plastic that has been molded into needlepoint canvas form. It comes in 7-, 10-, and 14-gauge, and is available in many colors that can be matched to the background color of your design. Plastic canvas never needs to be blocked, which makes it an excellent choice for small items like Christmas ornaments, or for items requiring a stiff or waterproof base, such as coasters, frames, placemats, and three-dimensional items. Plastic canvas has

been overlooked as a medium by serious needlepointers because the designs created for it have tended to be overly cute. I used plastic canvas in a number of the projects in this book, and everyone who has seen them had no idea that the underlying canvas was plastic until I told them! I began experimenting with it a few years ago and have been very pleased with the results: I hope you will try it with an open mind. You can substitute cotton canvas for any of my projects that use plastic canvas, but you will have to block the cotton canvas.

THREADS

WOOL

There are three standard types of wool available that can be used for needlepoint. If you wish to duplicate my needlepoint designs exactly as shown in this book, you should use the same colors and the same brand of wool or fibers that I used. You should also use the same size canvas that I used so that the piece will be the same finished size. Colors vary from brand to brand; if you do use an alternative yarn, the finished piece will not be exactly the same as my original design.

PERSIAN YARN

Made by Paternayan (called Paterna in Europe and Australia), DMC, Woolmasters, and others, Persian yarn comes as one strand consisting of three separate plies that have been twisted together (the word *"ply"* refers to the individual strands of yarn that can be easily pulled apart). With most Persian wool the three plies differ slightly in thickness: in each strand there's a "Papa" (the thickest), a "Mama" (medium thickness), and a "Baby" (the thinnest). If you are working on 12-gauge canvas, separate the plies and use 1 Papa-ply and 1 Baby-ply together, or use 2 Mama-plies in order to make evenly weighted strands. For 18-mesh, because the Baby-ply may be too thin to cover the canvas well, use only the Papa- and Mama-plies (you can save the Baby-plies for another project).

Depending on the mesh count of your cotton canvas, use the following wool amounts: 5 plies of Persian wool for 5-mesh and 4 plies for 7-mesh (these are good canvas gauges for rugs), 3 plies of Persian wool for 10-mesh, 2 plies for 12-mesh, 1 or 2 plies for 14-mesh (depending upon the thickness of the plies), and 1 ply for 18-mesh canvas.

Plastic canvas may require different amounts of Persian wool plies than cotton canvas. For example, 14-count plastic canvas takes 1 ply of Persian wool (Papa or Mama only) for 14-count mesh, 10-count plastic takes 2 plies, etc. It's best to do a test swatch to determine what you will need.

TAPESTRY YARN

Made by Elsa Williams, DMC, Rowan, Appleton, Anchor, and others, this yarn is a heavier weight wool, which means you can use 1 strand on 12-mesh canvas, 1 or 2 strands on 10-mesh, 2 to 3 strands on 7-mesh, and 3 to 4 strands on 5-mesh canvas. Tapestry wool is not suitable for use on finer mesh canvases such as 14- or 18-count because the plies cannot (and should not) be separated.

CREWEL YARN

Made by Paternayan, DMC, Appleton, and others, this fine, twisted 2-ply wool is thinner than Persian wool, but can be used for needlepoint. You need to use 3 strands together to cover 12-mesh canvas and 4 strands for 10-mesh canvas. It is a good idea to stitch a test swatch to determine how many threads you will need to use for your canvas. Crewel works very well on finer mesh canvases such as 14-, 18- or smaller gauges.

OTHER FIBERS

Needlepoint can also be stitched using embroidery floss, silk, metallic threads, pearl cotton, and rug yarn. I have used knitting wool successfully on 12-, 10-, and 7-mesh canvas; it simply requires a little experimenting to see if the weight of your knitting wool will work or "fill" your canvas properly. You want yarn that is thin enough to pass through the canvas holes without too much tugging, yet thick enough to cover the canvas well. Whatever wool you use should be tightly spun so that it won't fray as you stitch with it, and so that it will hold up well for years of wear as a pillow or a rug (a rug will get much harder wear than a pillow). This is a great way to use up extra wool you may have hiding in your closets!

When you select fibers, bear in mind what you plan to use the needlepoint for: needlepoint used to cover a chair seat or other furniture is best stitched in wool because wool is the hardest wearing fiber.

MIXING COLORS

Most of the fibers described here come in color "families" that include five or more graduated shades of a color that work well to create subtle shading. The great thing about Persian and crewel yarns (embroidery floss and silk, too) is that you can combine plies of two or more colors simultaneously in your needle as you stitch—these are wonderfully versatile fibers. You can also mix other yarns if your canvas gauge will accept the wool. The variety of possible color combinations is infinite, and mixing colors with needlepoint is endlessly exciting.

One of my favorite techniques is to use two very close shades of the same color in my needle: as you stitch you get a subtle "tweeding" effect that adds richness and depth to your needlepoint. Be brave and experiment with the fibers you have at hand. You can do small practice swatches first to see if you like the combination of colors, and then use it in your needlework.

COLORFASTNESS

Recently, stricter regulations have been imposed in America and Europe on all dye chemicals to make them less toxic to the environment. Wool dyed by reputable wool manufacturers seldom has problems with colors running, but due to the new FDA and EPA regulations, manufacturers now cannot guarantee complete colorfastness. The colors most likely to run are the red family. If you have any doubts, try overnight soaking of two good sized-sample pieces of the fiber you are using. Start one sample in very hot water and the other in cold water. If neither color bleeds into the water after an overnight soak then it should be colorfast and you can safely wet it for the blocking process.

NEEDLES

You should use a tapestry needle for needlepoint. It has a blunt point to glide smoothly between the threads of your canvas and a long eye (opening) that is large enough for yarn or multiple threads. The needle should be of good quality; this ensures that the inside of the eye will have been ground finely so that it does not catch or tear the fiber. As a general guide I use a size 18 needle for 10- and 12-mesh canvas. Tapestry needles come in a variety of sizes; you can determine what size you need from the chart below (if two sizes are given, the type/thickness of the fiber you use will determine which size is better):

CANVAS GAUGE / MESH	TAPESTRY NEEDLE SIZE
5 to the inch (cm)	#13 or #16
7 to the inch (cm)	#16
10 to the inch (cm)	#18
12 to the inch (cm)	#20
14 to the inch (cm)	#20 or #22
18 to the inch (cm)	#22 or #24
22 and 24 to the inch (cm)	#24 or #26

The equivalent mesh in plastic canvas may require slightly different needle sizes, depending upon whether the canvas holes are square or octagonal. I use a size 22 needle for 14-mesh plastic canvas.

SANTA AND FRIENDS TRAY, PAGE 86

FRAMES

I stitch all my needlepoint without a frame because this method makes my needlepoint more portable (bulky frames are really frowned upon in airplanes and trains!). I can roll up my needlepoint and do it in the garden or while waiting in line, and I can stitch using the "sewing" method which is twice as fast as the "stabbing" method. However, working without a frame means I always have to have my work blocked. The good news is that I get twice as much stitched!

The advantages to stitching on a frame are (1) you probably won't have to block your work, and (2) it can help beginners achieve an even stitch tension. Some people prefer working on a frame; my advice is to try stitching with and without one to see which way you prefer. If you decide to use a frame, there are many sizes and types to choose from; try several to see which is best for the result you want.

STITCHING METHODS

For all the needlepoint stitches described below there are two ways of stitching—the "sewing" or "scooping" method and the "stab-stitching" method. With the sewing method, you use one smooth motion to scoop your needle under the threads of the canvas and then up—ready for the next stitch. Because you use only one motion per stitch, you can stitch two pieces of needlepoint in the time it would take to stitch one piece on a frame using the stab-stitching method. When using the sewing method, you need to be careful not to catch any part of adjacent stitches into the stitch you are currently sewing.

If your needlepoint is on a frame, you pretty much have to use the stab-stitching method: this means you pull the needle down through the canvas in one motion, and then you draw it back up through the canvas in the second motion. You must make two motions for each stitch. If you plan to enter your needlepoint in a competition, then you should use the stab-stitching method because your stitches will be cleaner, which is something judges look for. But if you are just stitching for your own pleasure, the finished look between the two methods is nearly imperceptible. Some people claim that if you stretch your needlepoint loosely on a frame you can use the sewing method...I've never done it successfully myself, which is why I work without a frame using the sewing method.

NEEDLEPOINT STITCHES

There are many types of stitches used in needlepoint to achieve different effects. But the three basic stitches are half-cross, continental or tent, and basketweave. Just to confuse things, in England these stitches may all be referred to as tent stitches and are worked in half-cross, continental, or basketweave techniques.

All three stitches look identical on the front of a needlepoint canvas because all the stitches lie in the same direction: the bottom of each stitch is in the lower left corner and the top of each stitch is in the upper right corner. However, the back sides of each stitch look very different from one another. Moreover, each type of stitch has its appropriate use. If you aren't sure which one to use, I suggest you use the continental stitch. It is easy to work and is good for both filling background and for stitching the details of your design. However, if you haven't tried all three stitches, it is a good idea to do so to see which one you prefer.

HALF-CROSS STITCH

Half-cross stitch is easy to learn, easy to stitch, and uses 30 to 35 percent less wool than either continental or basketweave stitches. However, because it forms only short vertical stitches on the back, this stitch does not cover and protect the back of your work well. Moreover, half-cross stitches distort a canvas, making it necessary to block the finished piece. This may not be a problem for a pillow, but may be a problem for a chair seat or rug that gets hard wear.

Half-cross is a tight stitch and doesn't leave a lot of space to run the ends of your threads through the back of the stitches. If you use the half-cross stitch, you must stitch all the rows in your piece either horizontally or vertically. If you try to stitch some areas horizontally and some areas vertically, you will see vertical and horizontal ridges in your work which is not attractive, and, unfortunately, the ridges will not disappear after your piece is blocked.

Although I began doing needlepoint with this stitch, I now use only continental or basketweave stitches for my work.

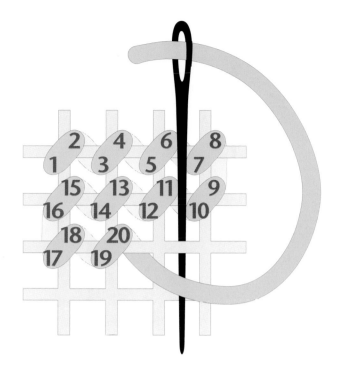

CONTINENTAL STITCH

Continental stitch is easy to learn and relatively easy to stitch. Unlike half-cross stitch, you can stitch some areas using the continental stitch horizontally and some areas vertically in the same piece, and it will all look smooth and even on the front (with no ridges). As a result, the continental stitch is very flexible—you can stitch a small area here and a small area there all over the canvas until you've filled everything in. The back of the work is durable and wears well. And because the stitches are longer on the backside, it is easy to run the ends of your threads through the backside of your stitches. However, this stitch will distort your canvas and your finished work will need to be blocked.

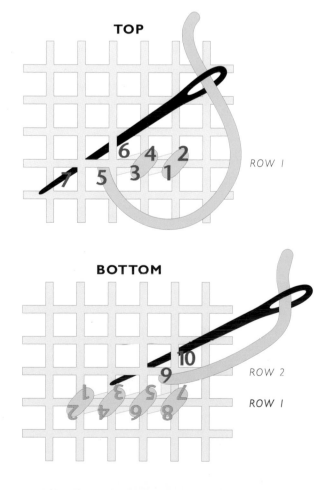

TOP

ROW 1

BOTTOM

ROW 2

ROW 1

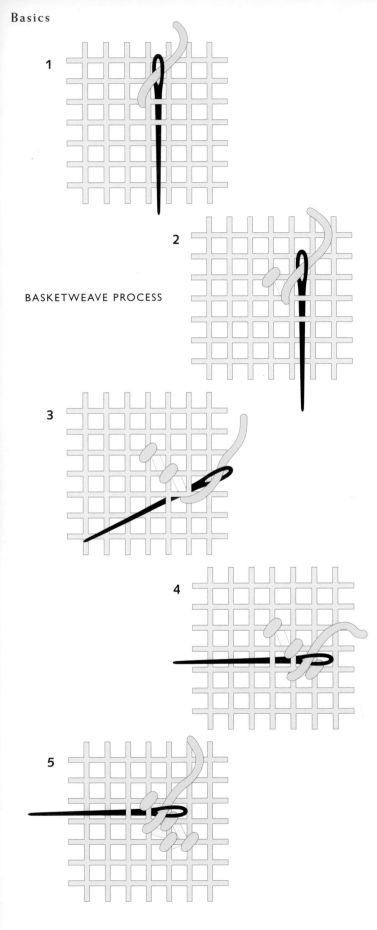

1

2

BASKETWEAVE PROCESS

3

4

5

BASKETWEAVE

Basketweave stitch is relatively easy to learn but somewhat difficult to stitch (it requires some practice to get used to the technique). Because basketweave must be stitched in diagonal rows, it is best to start in one corner and work your way down (or up) in the same direction across the entire piece. This stitch is best for larger areas and not easy to do if you have very small design areas to stitch. Regarding the latter case, I (and many other people) use continental for the small areas and basketweave to fill in the background. For strength and durability, basketweave is unrivalled—this stitch creates a thick, long-wearing back. It will distort your canvas very little, so blocking (if needed) is relatively easy.

RIGHT-HANDED VERSUS LEFT-HANDED STITCHING

Almost all stitching diagrams are drawn assuming use by a right-handed person. However, you can easily adapt them for left-handed use. If you use the stab-stitching method, you can follow the same diagrams as right-handed people without any changes. If you sew or scoop, simply turn the diagrams upside down, turn your work upside down, then follow the numbers on the diagrams, working with your left hand. Your work will look the same as right-handed work when you are finished.

GENERAL STITCHING INSTRUCTIONS

LIGHTING

Before you begin stitching, be sure you will be working in a comfortable situation with good light. I use a standing, hooded halogen lamp that produces 500 watts, which is like having bright daylight when I stitch in the evening. However, if I have to match or select wool colors, I do so only during daylight hours because colors look radically different under artificial light. Daylight simulation light bulbs are now available which I am told are wonderful if you are working with colors of similar shades.

CONVERTING CANVAS SIZES

Let's say you want to stitch a design from this book to fit a particular chair you own, but the finished dimensions of the design are too small (or too large). You can enlarge or reduce any of the designs in this book simply by changing the size of the canvas you use. For example, let's say that the design you like is 180 stitches wide and 180 stitches high when stitched on 12-mesh canvas—this equals a 15-inch (38 cm) square. If you stitch this design (still 180 by 180 stitches) on a 10-mesh canvas, the design would measure 18 by 18 inches (45 by 45 cm). And if you used a 7-mesh canvas, the same design would measure 25¾ inches (65 cm) square!

The way you can calculate this is to take the dimension in stitches and divide it by the canvas mesh count: 180 stitches divided by 12 = 15, or 15 inches (38 cm); 180 stitches divided by 10 = 18, or 18 inches (45 cm), and so on. This is a very easy way to enlarge or reduce designs to end up with just the size you want—without having to alter the charted design whatsoever!

MARKING YOUR CANVAS

Before you start to stitch your design, it's important to write the word "top" on the tape at the top of your canvas. This is helpful because when you use some stitches you will have to turn the canvas upside down, which may confuse you, especially if you are stitching geometric patterns that do not have an obvious top! Always use a *waterproof marker or pen*, and *never mark the canvas itself with regular ink* because it may not be colorfast. You can buy waterproof pens in a variety of colors for lightly marking the canvas—be sure to test any waterproof pen by marking a scrap piece of canvas. Let it dry and then rub it vigorously. You should also immerse the inked canvas scrap in water and rub it again. If the ink doesn't rub off or bleed into the water, then you can use that pen to mark your canvas. I suggest you use ink colors that will match (approximately) the colors in your design; they will be much easier to follow that way.

Before you start to stitch, you also need to mark the outside dimensions of the needlepoint design onto the canvas. Be sure to allow an extra unstitched border of 2 to 3 inches (5 to 7.5 cm) all around the needlepoint design. Fold the canvas in half in both directions to find the center point and, with your waterproof pen, mark the center lines both vertically and horizontally. This divides the design into quarters which makes it easier to count. Now mark your canvas with the outside dimensions of the design. Count the canvas *threads* (not the holes) to determine the size of the charted design area (the number of stitches for height and width are indicated in the instructions for each needlepoint design). I find it easier to start in the middle and count out the right half of the design, then return to the middle and count out the left half.

PREPARING TO STITCH

You may find it helpful to bind the edges of the canvas with 1-inch-wide (2.5 cm) white pressure tape or strapping tape to prevent the rough edges from catching the needlepoint wool

and your clothing. You can also use masking tape, but don't leave it on the canvas for more than a few weeks or expose the tape to high heat as it can leave glue on the canvas. Your hands must be clean and free of any hand lotion because dirt and oil will rub off on your work.

STITCHING

It is a good idea to "strip" or "ply" the strands of your Persian yarn or embroidery floss before stitching. This will fluff out the individual plies and make the fibers cover the canvas more smoothly and evenly. To strip/ply your fibers, separate them into individual plies, then put together as many as you need and thread your needle with them. To thread your needle, use a needle threader or double over the end of the yarn, press it lightly between thumb and forefinger, and insert it in the eye of the needle. If your wool becomes twisted as you stitch, let the needle dangle from the canvas and untwist itself. If you do this often your work will be smoother and more even overall.

Try to maintain an even tension and try not to pull the stitches too tightly, or the canvas will show through and the work will twist out of shape. Do not take or "carry" the wool from one area of color to another of the same color unless those areas are adjacent—within 5 to 6 stitches in any direction. Stitch the design details first, and then fill in the background. Wherever possible, work the lightest colors first; this avoids the catching and stitching in of any dark-colored hairs from other dark stitches which will show in the lighter colored stitches.

STARTING AND FINISHING A LENGTH OF THREAD

When you stitch, use short lengths, such as 22 to 32 inches (56 to 81 cm); this will help keep the wool from fraying as you work. If you are using floss or metallic threads, use a shorter length of 15 to 20 inches (38 to 50 cm). Use this shorter length, too, when working on finer (smaller gauge) canvases, because with smaller stitches the fibers will be pulled through the canvas even more often.

When you begin a strand of wool, bring the needle through from the back of the canvas and leave 2 inches (5 cm) of wool hanging free at the back of the canvas. Once you come to the end of your strand of wool, run it through the back of 7 to 10 horizontal or vertical stitches (do not go back through stitches diagonally) that you have just completed. Do this for the 2-inch (5 cm) tail that you left hanging free and for all other strands used in order to prevent any stitches from becoming loose.

Wherever possible, run the ends of your threads back through the same color as the thread itself. This is especially important when using dark threads; if you run a dark thread under the back of a light thread, it may show through on the front of your work. Your finished piece may become a family heirloom, so do sign and date it for the pleasure of future family members and friends. You and they should be proud of your beautiful work!

STITCHING FROM A CHART

The advantage of working needlepoint from a chart is seeing your blank canvas blossom with color as your design grows. Those of you who prefer to work on a printed canvas will be pleased to find that some of the designs featured in this book are available as kits (see page 124).

When working with a chart, the first thing to do is *match all your fiber colors to the corresponding symbols on the color key*. This is an important step because sometimes, in order to make printed charts easier to read, it is necessary to slightly exaggerate the printed colors. In fact, in my book many of the colors in the charts are lighter than the actual wool.

Working from a chart is not at all difficult—it just requires careful counting. Note that each square on the chart represents one stitch on your canvas, and the color/symbol indicates which fiber to use. You simply count the number of squares of a particular color on the chart, then work this number of stitches onto the canvas. You should always count the *threads* of the canvas and *not the holes*. The color key near the chart provides the exact fiber to use; you should also refer to the photograph.

Where you start the design is really a matter of personal preference. You can start in the middle, at the top or bottom, or you can stitch some of the design here and there at random. Be sure that the top of your needlepoint corresponds to the top of the chart (the top of the chart is always at the top of the page in this book). As long as it is for your own personal use only, I suggest that you photocopy and enlarge the chart you are working on. That way you can make notes on the photocopy and draw lines through each row or section you have stitched as an easy way to keep track of where you are working. If the chart is split into two or more pages, you can keep them separate or tape them together—whatever you find easier.

FINISHING

BLOCKING / STRETCHING THE CANVAS

If your canvas has pulled out of shape when completely stitched, it must be blocked before the piece can be finished as a pillow or other item. This means it must be dampened and stretched as follows to make it square again:

1. Take a piece of board (plywood, chipboard, or fiberboard) several inches larger than the completed piece of canvas and mark the exact dimensions of your piece as outlines on the board (be sure the corners are all right angles). Cover the board with transparent plastic wrap.

2. Place the canvas face downwards with the worked edges meeting the marked shape. Secure all sides of the canvas to the board by using rustproof staples, tacks, or nails spaced ¼ inch (1 cm) apart, stretching and pulling the work until it lines up with the outlines on the board and is squared, with the warp (horizontal) and weft (vertical) threads at right angles to each other. You can lightly dampen the back of the entire canvas, using only a damp cloth or sponge with *cool water*, in order to allow for enough stretching to bring the piece back into square. Do not soak the needlepoint and do

not use an iron or a steamer (soaking, hot water and/or concentrated heat/steam could cause the wool colors to run).

3. A sizing agent (such as wallpaper paste or starch paste) may be applied to the back of the piece to assure that the stretched piece will remain permanently square. I do this for all my needlepoint. However, before using it on the entire piece, be sure to *test it first* on a separate sample swatch of stitched needlepoint.

Apply enough paste to penetrate the fibers somewhat, however do not put on so much paste that it seeps through to the front of the piece, and *do not leave a lot of excess paste on the back*. Allow the canvas several days to dry thoroughly. When dry, remove the tacks and finish as directed.

CLEANING NEEDLEPOINT

It is important to regard needlepoint as a type of thick woolen upholstery fabric that requires specialized care. In general, when the piece needs cleaning, take it to a professional dry cleaner who has experience with handling and cleaning needlework. If you have used paste to block your needlework, alert the cleaner to this *before* the piece is cleaned!

ANIMALS

Chapter 1

THE STORY OF NOAH'S ARK IS IRRESISTIBLE

and was great fun to translate into needlepoint. Because I couldn't include all the animals in the world, I decided to feature a few animals native to North America, such as skunks and beavers. I rounded them out with my favorites from other continents.

NOAH'S ARK PILLOW

FINISHED MEASUREMENTS

- 16½ x 16¼ inches (42 x 41.5 cm)
- 198 stitches wide x 195 stitches high

MATERIALS

- 10 colors of Paternayan wool
- 12-mesh cotton canvas 21 x 21 inches (54 x 54 cm)
- Size 18 tapestry needle
- Finishing accessories: twisted cord, zipper, backing fabric, pillow form

WORKING THE DESIGN

Use continental stitch throughout with 2 strands of Paternayan wool in your needle.

FINISHING

Trim the edges of the canvas to within 1 inch (2.5 cm) of the needlepoint stitches. Choose the color of your backing fabric carefully—you do not want it to over-whelm the needlepoint. If you are in doubt, find a color that matches the back-ground color of your needlepoint. Using a piece of the backing fabric cut to the same size as the trimmed needlepoint, place back and front pieces with right sides together and stitch between the first and second row of needlepoint stitches, leaving an opening on one side for inserting the pillow filling. Turn the pillow right side out, insert the pillow filling, turn the edges of the opening, and slip stitch together (or put in a zipper). If desired, sew twisted cord trim over the seam that joins the pil-low to the backing fabric.

Noah's Ark Pillow

PATERNAYAN PERSIAN WOOLS

Symbol	№	Color	Yards	Meters
/	530	Dark Spruce	10	9
\	611	Grass Green	45	41
И	454	Khaki	27	25
K	262	White	40	37
B	480	Terracotta	27	25
–	542	Sky Blue	80	73
●	725	Yellow	18	17
H	540	Cobalt Blue	55	50
I	969	Red	27	25
■	420	Dark Brown	36	33

DESIGNER TIP

You can create other projects using selected elements in this design. For example, the two elephants could be used to stitch a box top; a row of animals (either one animal repeated or a variety of animals) could be stitched to fashion a belt.

I LEARNED WHAT A CHARMING SUBJECT PIGS COULD BE *when a client commissioned me to create a piece as a Christmas present for her friend who is an avid collector of pig novelties. These happy springtime pigs are a variation of that commissioned design. Because the pattern is intended for a small box top, it can be stitched in just a few evenings.*

PIG BOX TOP

FINISHED MEASUREMENTS

- 4½ x 9 inches (11 x 23 cm)
- 51 stitches high x 107 stitches wide

MATERIALS

- 10 colors of Paternayan wool
- 12-mesh cotton canvas 7½ x 13 inches (19 x 33 cm)
- Size 18 tapestry needle
- Finishing accessories: box from Creative Furnishings. See supplier list on page 124.

WORKING THE DESIGN

Use continental stitch throughout with 2 strands of Paternayan wool in your needle.

FINISHING

I used Creative Furnishing's TBO Oblong Box; you could also use Sudberry Houses' Long Pencil Box if you added 5 to 6 extra stitched rows to the outside edge of the design.

On the underside of the padded top, measure and mark the center point on all four sides. Lay the needlepoint canvas over the padded top, matching the center points of your needlepoint canvas to the center points marked on the underside of the padded top so that the needlepoint equally covers the top and extends a little bit under the underside. Staple gun or nail all four center points. Then, working from the center, attach the needlepoint so that it evenly covers the top and sides of the padded top. Gently press the top so that it slides into the opening of the box top. Open the lid and secure the padded top to the lid with the screw provided. If the screw is too short, you may need to buy a longer one to make sure it securely holds the top to the lid.

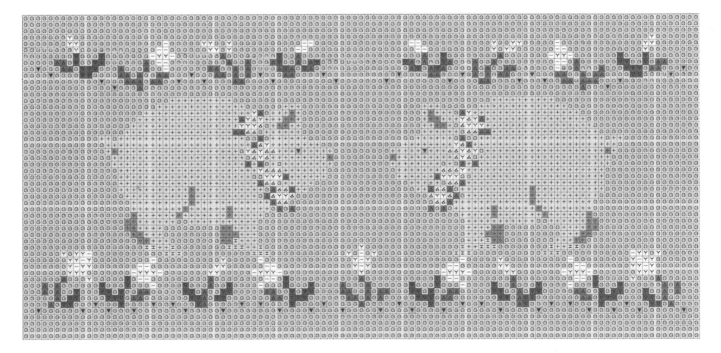

Pig Box Top

PATERNAYAN PERSIAN WOOLS

Symbol	№	Color	Yards	Meters	Symbol	№	Color	Yards	Meters
—	262	Creamy White	6	6	+	946	Pink	12	11
Y	773	Sunny Yellow	6	6	▽	661	Dark Green	7	6
6	771	Deep Yellow	3	3	△	662	Med. Green	9	8
▼	544	Sky Blue	4	4	G	664	Pale Green (BKGD)	50	46
◦◦◦	932	Dusty Rose	4	4	I	454	Khaki Brown	2	2

ANIMAL PRINTS ARE ALWAYS IN FASHION, *and this is a particularly versatile design. Here I've included two stitched examples of the same size—one finished as an eyeglass case and one as a trivet. You can also finish it as a checkbook cover or a small pillow.*

LEOPARD SKIN EYEGLASS CASE & TRIVET

FINISHED MEASUREMENTS

- 7 x 7 inches (18 x 18 cm)
- 70 stitches wide x 70 stitches high

MATERIALS

- 5 colors of Paternayan wool
- 10-mesh cotton canvas 11 x 11 inches (28 x 28 cm)
- Size 18 tapestry needle
- Finishing accessories: FOR EYEGLASS CASE—lining fabric
  FOR TRIVET—1 thin piece of balsa wood, 7 x 7 inches (18 x 18 cm)
  FOR BOTH—1 yard (.9 m) thin black twisted cord

WORKING THE DESIGN

Use continental stitch throughout with 3 strands of
Paternayan wool in your needle.

FINISHING THE EYEGLASS CASE

Trim the unstitched edges of the needlepoint to ½ inch (1.3 cm). Fold down one
side and baste it to form the eyeglass case
opening. Then, with right sides facing
inward, fold the needlepoint in half and
sew the bottom seam and the long seam,
leaving the basted top end open. Turn
the eyeglass case right side out. To finish
the seams nicely, sew thin black twisted
cord over the bottom and side seams and
around the top opening. Line the case
with velveteen or soft flannel to protect
the eyeglass lenses.

FINISHING THE TRIVET

Cut a thin piece of balsa wood ¼ inch (1 cm) smaller on all sides than the stitched trivet. Fold the needlepoint over the board and, with thick thread and needle, lace the top side to the bottom side so that none of the blank canvas is showing. Then repeat the same thing for the right and left sides. Cover the edges with thin black twisted cording. To better protect the needlepoint, you can order a plastic trivet cover from Fond Memories (see supplier list on page 124).

Leopard Skin
Eyeglass Case & Trivet

PATERNAYAN PERSIAN WOOL

Symbol	№	Color	Yards	Meters	
•	220	Black	35	32	
1	733	Light Gold	8	7	
2	750	Golden Brown	20	18	
3	496 & 732*		15	14	of each color

Mix 1 strand of #496 with 2 strands of #732

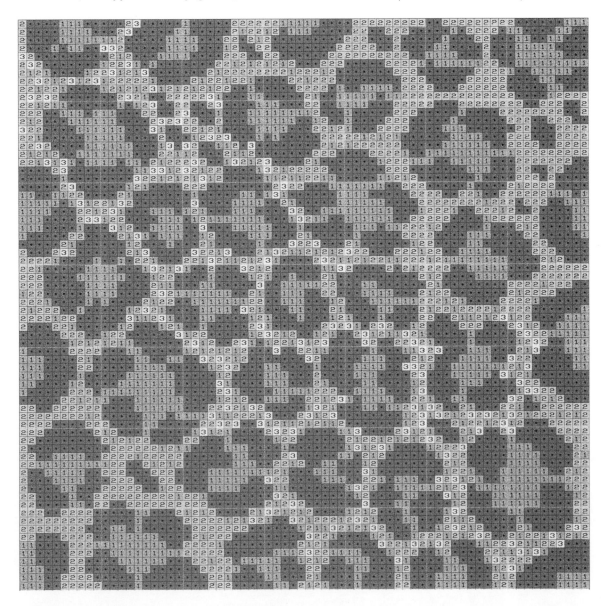

IN MEDIEVAL TAPESTRIES, WHICH PROVIDED THE INSPIRATION FOR THIS DESIGN, *wild animals such as foxes were usually being hunted, so they appear gaunt and pretty miserable looking! I used flowers from the Cluny Tapestries but made my fox contented and well fed. My fox dreams of nice things as he snoozes peacefully in a thicket of fragrant flowers.*

MEDIEVAL FOX PILLOW

FINISHED MEASUREMENTS

- 16½ x 16¾ inches (42.5 x 43 cm)
- 201 stitches wide x 198 stitches high

MATERIALS

- 10 colors of Paternayan wool
- 12-mesh cotton canvas 21 x 21 inches (53 x 53 cm)
- Size 18 tapestry needle
- Finishing accessories: twisted cord, zipper, backing fabric, pillow form

WORKING THE DESIGN

Use continental stitch throughout with 2 strands of Paternayan wool in your needle.

FINISHING

Trim the edges of the canvas to within 1 inch (2.5 cm) of the needlepoint stitches. Choose the color of your backing fabric carefully—you do not want it to overwhelm the needlepoint. If you are in doubt, find a color that matches the background color of your needlepoint. Using a piece of the backing fabric cut to the same size as the trimmed needlepoint, place back and front pieces with right sides together and stitch between the first and second row of needlepoint stitches, leaving an opening on one side for inserting the pillow filling. Turn the pillow right side out, insert the pillow filling, turn the edges of the opening, and slip stitch together (or put in a zipper). If desired, sew twisted cord trim over the seam that joins the pillow to the backing fabric.

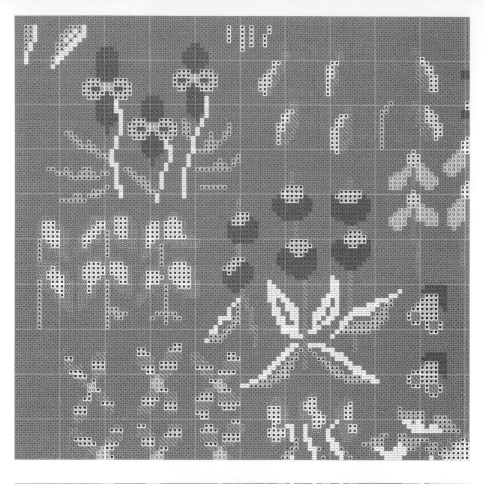

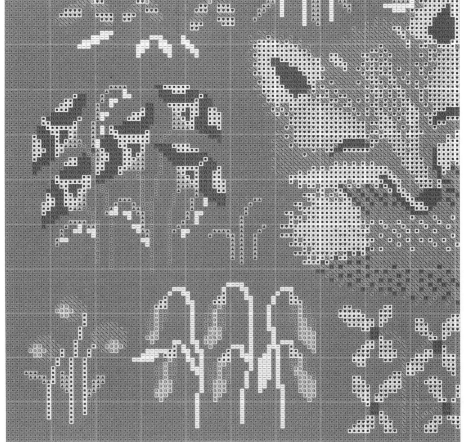

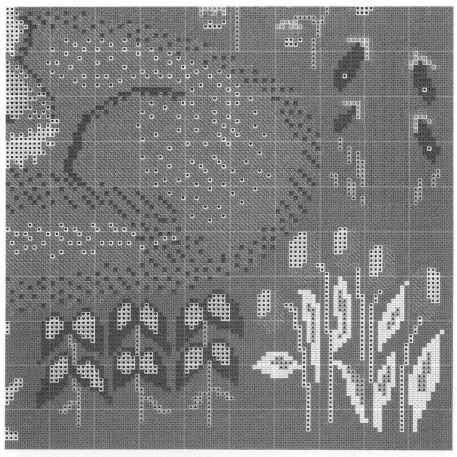

Medieval Fox Pillow

PATERNAYAN PERSIAN WOOLS

Symbol	№	Color	Yards	Meters
▲	602	Med. Green	40	37
◙	499	Pale Apricot	40	37
▼	497	Med. Apricot	40	37
−	653	Pale Green	40	37
+	600	Dark Green	40	37
\	495	Dark Apricot	80	73
O	513	Medium Blue	40	37
B	515	Pale Blue	40	37
•	571	Navy Blue (BKGD)	280	256
R	870	Rusty Brown	40	37

To make the Fox Pillow with the red background: substitute #930 for #571, and #400 for #870.

DESIGNER TIP

Both the navy blue and brick red background colors were used in medieval tapestries. If you favor red, simply substitute it for the navy blue background stitches (and substitute brown as listed above) as shown in chart.

THIS SIMPLE PROJECT IS AN EFFECTIVE USE OF PATTERN REPETITION *(Panda-monium!). To make the snow more interesting I intentionally stitched the snowflakes going in all directions (sideways, backwards, upside down, etc.) on top of the red background. This is definitely an unorthodox way to stitch, but I was pleased with the effect.*

PANDA BEAR PINCUSHION

FINISHED MEASUREMENTS
- 6 x 6 inches (15 x 15 cm)
- 74 stitches wide x 72 stitches high

MATERIALS
- 3 colors of Paternayan wool
- 12-mesh cotton canvas 10 x 10 inches (25 x 25 cm)
- Size 18 tapestry needle
- Finishing accessories: backing fabric, pillow filling, 1 yard (.9 m) each black and white bobble trim presewn on tape

WORKING THE DESIGN

Use continental stitch throughout with 2 strands of Paternayan wool in your needle. Stitch some of the white dots over the red background sideways, backwards, and vertically to make the dots vary in direction.

FINISHING

Trim the edges of the canvas to within 1 inch (2.5 cm) of the needlepoint stitches. Choose the color of your backing fabric carefully—you do not want it to overwhelm the needlepoint. If you are in doubt, find a color that matches the background color of your needlepoint. Use a piece of the backing fabric cut to the same size as the trimmed needlepoint. Sandwich the bobble tape (offset so that every other bobble is white) between the back and front pieces—right sides together—and stitch between the first and second row of needlepoint stitches, leaving an opening on one side to insert the filling. Turn the pincushion right side out, insert the filling, turn the edges of the opening, and slip stitch together.

Panda Bear Pincushion

PATERNAYAN PERSIAN WOOLS

Symbol	№	Color	Yards	Meters
■	220	Black	20	18
−	260	White	20	18
■	969	Red	30	27

Uncle bear sports a jaunty vest depicting some of his favorite things—trout, honey, blue and red berries, and his other bear pals. This is an easy project because you can stitch it on a premade blank vest (see supplier information for the vest and bears). This vest could certainly be worn by other stuffed animals or dolls (assuming that Uncle Bear gives you his permission).

TEDDY BEAR VEST

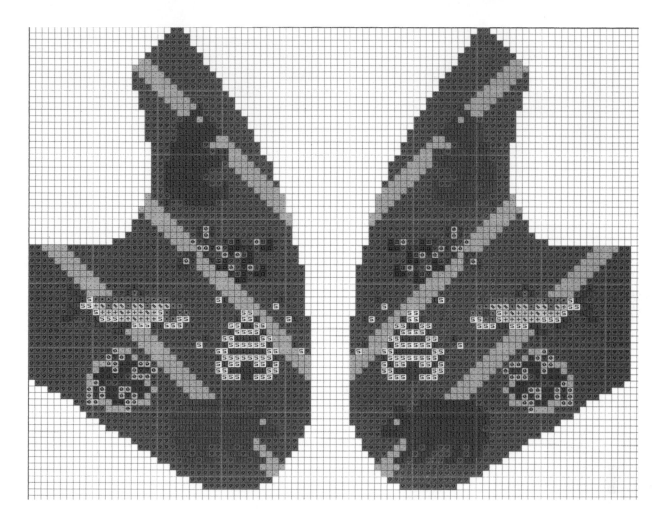

FINISHED MEASUREMENTS OF EACH VEST PIECE

- 3 x 5 inches (7.5 x 13 cm)
- Each vest piece is 44 stitches wide x 72 stitches high

MATERIALS

- 13 colors of Paternayan wool
- One blank prefinished vest (14-mesh cotton canvas)
- Size 22 tapestry needle
- Finishing accessories: pre-finished vest. See supplier list on page 124.

WORKING THE DESIGN

Use 2 strands of Paternayan wool in your needle.

FINISHING

It's important to note that this vest comes preassembled. To avoid the need for any blocking, the vest must be stitched in basketweave. If you like, to cover the inside of the needlepoint vest fronts, you could baste small pieces of lightweight fabric to the inside halves of the vest. Do not wet the synthetic suede backing of the vest, as it may not be colorfast.

Teddy Bear Vest

Symbol	№	Color	Yards	Meters
	211	Dark Pearl Grey	2	2
	212	Pearl Grey	2	2
	430	Chocolate Brown	7	6
	401	Fawn Brown	7	6
5	727	Pale Yellow	3	3
	500	Federal Blue	2	2
	543	Sky Blue (BKGD)	30	27
	544	Light Sky Blue	10	9
+	863	Light Copper	2	2
	969	Christmas Red	3	3
	852	Saffron	3	3
	690	Loden Green	3	3
	692	Light Loden Green	5	5

PATERNAYAN PERSIAN WOOLS

I AM A CAT LOVER, SO CAT PROJECTS WERE A MUST! *I've stitched my cat designs using a variety of fibers and color combinations to show you a few possibilities and to give you some ideas. Feel free to substitute colors that tie in with your own color scheme. By stitching the background in Christmas colors, you can make perfect cat ornaments for your tree.*

CAT REFRIGERATOR MAGNETS

"SOCKS"

FINISHED MEASUREMENTS

- 2½ x 3¼ inches (6.5 x 8.5 cm)
- 35 stitches wide x 46 stitches high

MATERIALS

- 3 colors of Paternayan wool or metallics (or Anchor floss for background)
- 14-mesh plastic canvas 3 x 4 inches (8 x 10 cm)
- Size 22 tapestry needle
- Finishing accessories: felt or synthetic suede for backing, magnets

WORKING THE DESIGN

Use continental stitch throughout with 1 strand of Paternayan wool, 2 strands of Madeira 'Glamour', 1 strand of Madeira 'Decora', and 6 strands of floss. To create the pupil of the cat's eye, use 1 ply of Paternayan #421 (dark brown) and stitch over the middle stitch in the eye. Finishing instructions are on page 43.

"Socks"

Symbol	№	Color		Yards	Meters
PATERNAYAN PERSIAN WOOL					
H	612	Grass Green	(BKGD)	4	4
T	261	White	(BKGD)	4	4
■	421	Very Dark Brown		4	4

METALLIC VERSION

Symbol	№	Color		Amount
MADEIRA 'DECORA'				
T	1482	White	(BKGD)	1 package
MADEIRA 'GLAMOUR'				
H	2415	Magenta	(BKGD)	1 spool
■	2412	Deep Purple		1 spool

ALTERNATIVE BACKGROUND COLORS

Symbol	№	Color		Amount
ANCHOR FLOSS				
T	305	Yellow	(BKGD)	1 skein
H	329	Orange	(BKGD)	1 skein

GRAY TABBY CAT

FINISHED MEASUREMENTS

- 3¼ x 3½ inches (8.5 x 9 cm)
- 45 stitches wide x 49 stitches high

MATERIALS

- 6 colors of Paternayan wool (or floss for background)
- 14-mesh plastic canvas 4 x 4 inches (10 x 10 cm)
- Size 22 tapestry needle
- Finishing accessories: felt or synthetic suede for backing, magnets

WORKING THE DESIGN

Use continental stitch throughout with 1 strand of Paternayan wool and 6 strands of floss in your needle. To create the pupils of the Tabby Cat's eyes, use 1 ply of Paternayan #221 (dark gray) and stitch over the middle stitch in each cat eye. Finishing instructions are on page 43.

Gray Tabby Cat

Symbol	№	Color		Yards	Meters
		PATERNAYAN PERSIAN WOOL			
♥	200	Med. Gray		3	3
G	202	Light Gray		4	4
●	497	Medium Orange		1	1
H	612	Grass Green	(BKGD)	4	4
T	261	White	(BKGD)	4	4
■	221	Dark Gray		4	4

ALTERNATIVE BACKGROUND COLORS

				DMC FLOSS	
T	353	Light Rose	(BKGD)	1 skein	
H	3712	Rose	(BKGD)	1 skein	

SIAMESE CAT

FINISHED MEASUREMENTS

- 3 x 3 inches (7.5 x 7.5 cm)
- 43 stitches wide x 44 stitches high

MATERIALS

- 5 colors of Paternayan wool
  (or pearl cotton for background)
- 14-mesh plastic canvas 4 x 4 inches (10 x 10 cm)
- Size 22 tapestry needle
- Finishing accessories: felt or synthetic suede for
  backing, magnets

WORKING THE DESIGN

Use continental stitch throughout with 1 strand of
Paternayan wool or pearl cotton #5 in your needle. To
create the pupils of the Siamese Cat's eyes, use 1 ply of
Paternayan #421 (brown) and make 1 vertical stitch
between the 2 green stitches of each eye. Finishing
instructions are on page 43.

Siamese Cat

Symbol	№	Color		Yards	Meters
		PATERNAYAN PERSIAN WOOL			
◇	475	Light Beige		2	2
●	421	Dark Brown		2	2
H	612	Grass Green	(BKGD)	4	4
T	261	White	(BKGD)	4	4
■	473	Med. Beige		2	2

ALTERNATIVE BACKGROUND COLORS

Symbol	№	Color		Yards
		DMC PERLE		
T	340	Lavender	(BKGD)	1 skein
H	333	Dk. Lavender	(BKGD)	1 skein

FINISHING ALL THE CATS

You can leave the backs unfinished or you can finish them by gluing a piece of felt or synthetic suede (trimmed so that it is slightly smaller than the magnet) to the back of the stitched piece. Then glue a 1-inch (2.5 cm) round or square magnet to the back center of the needlepoint and allow it to completely dry before using. You can also sew them to a ribbon to make a vertical wall hanging as shown at left.

DESIGNER TIP

There are many fuzzy-textured fibers available today that you could use to give the cat's coat a furry texture.

THIS IS MY FIRST SAMPLER DESIGN. *After I stitched the flowers for the Fox (page 29) I thought they would be adorable in miniature. Samplers are traditionally done in cross-stitch but they translate beautifully into needlepoint. I love bunnies so I included a pair for good luck.*

MILLE FLEUR SAMPLER

FINISHED MEASUREMENTS

- 13 x 15 inches (33 x 38 cm)
- 157 stitches wide x 180 stitches high

MATERIALS

- 10 colors of Paternayan Wool
- 12-mesh cotton canvas 17 x 19 inches (43 x 48 cm)
- Size 18 tapestry needle

WORKING THE DESIGN

Use continental stitch throughout with 2 strands of Paternayan wool in your needle.

FINISHING

I strongly advise you to have your needlepoint professionally framed. See supplier list on page 124.

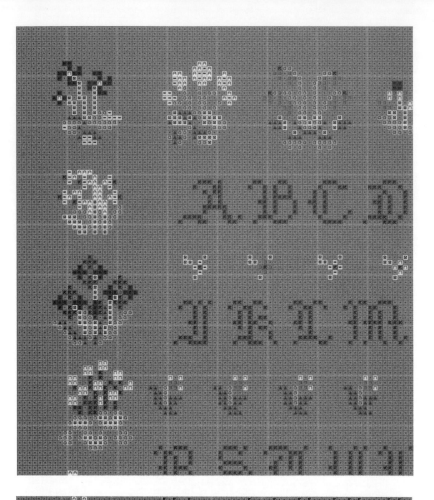

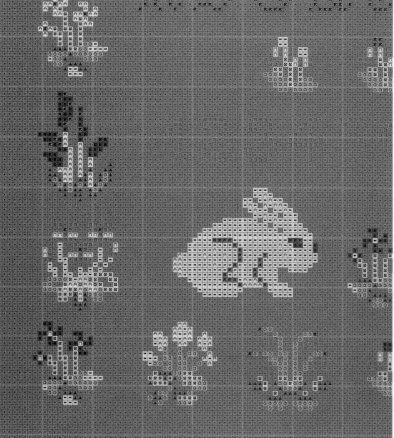

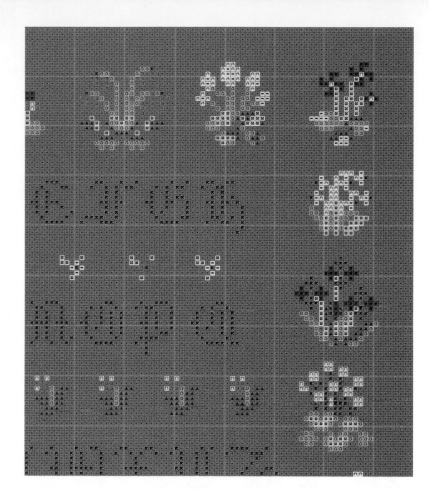

Mille Fleur Sampler

PATERNAYAN PERSIAN WOOLS

Symbol	№	Color	Yards	Meters
	870	Rusty Brown	40	37
K	495	Dark Apricot	40	37
▬	497	Med. Apricot	40	37
A	499	Pale Apricot	40	37
•	571	Navy Blue (BKGD)	240	220
∃	513	Medium Blue	40	37
∏	515	Pale Blue	40	37
G	602	Med. Green	40	37
▲	600	Dark Green	40	37
⊠	653	Pale Green	40	37

DESIGNER TIP

To protect your needlework, be sure your framer uses acid-free materials. Chemicals in acidic mat can leach into the needlework wool and cause irreparable damage over time.

HORSE & COW DOORSTOP

I'VE SHOWN THIS PROJECT AS A DOORSTOP

but it would also make an attractive paperweight. I used a fiber called Watercolors for all the backgrounds in this piece (see supplier information). It is exciting to work with because the fiber changes color as you stitch and creates surprising and striking color combinations. I like leaving the ends of the brick showing. The effect is attractive and the piece is much easier to finish.

FINISHED MEASUREMENTS

- 6 x 12 inches (15 x 30 cm)
- 60 stitches wide x 120 stitches high

MATERIALS

- 13 colors of Caron Watercolors and Paternayan wool
- 10-mesh cotton canvas 10 x 16 inches (25 x 40 cm)
- Size 18 tapestry needle
- Finishing accessories: twisted cord, a brick

WORKING THE DESIGN

Use basketweave stitch throughout with 3 strands of Paternayan wool and 1 (3-ply) strand of Caron Watercolors.

FINISHING

Fold the left-and right-side edges of the needlepoint under and baste them securely. Sew twisted cord to the left and right sides, leaving 1 inch (2.5 cm) of extra cording at each end. Then take the needlepoint piece and wrap it around the brick, leaving equal portions of the brick exposed on both ends. Sew the needlepoint top and bottom edges together so that the piece snugly surrounds the brick. Neatly tuck the cording ends under and tack stitch them to form two continuous corded edges.

Horse & Cow Doorstop

PATERNAYAN PERSIAN WOOLS

Symbol	№	Color	Yards	Meters
•	221	Charcoal	2	2
◣	220	Black	18	17
W	261	White	9	8
▮	420	Dark Brown	7	6
●	401	Med. Brown	17	16
2	402	Light Brown	2	2
+	835	Pink	2	2

CARON WATERCOLORS

∧	Crystal Bay	1 skein	
≑	Burnt Toast	1 skein	
▽	Emerald	2 skeins	
⊖	Jade	2 skeins	
◤	Amethyst	2 skeins	
∥	Delphinium	1 skein	

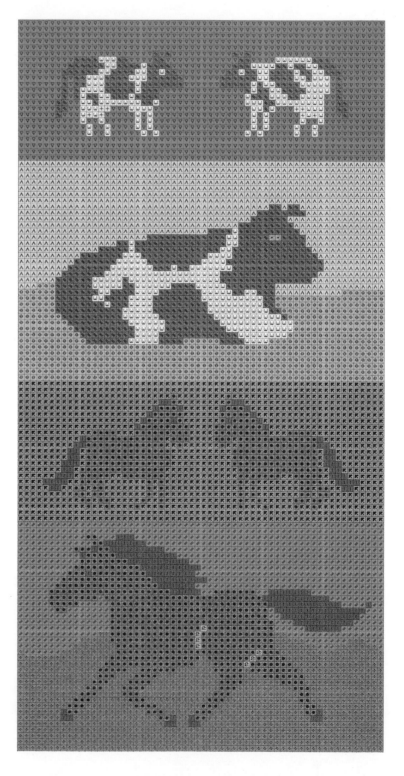

FLOWERS, FRUIT, and TEXTILES

Chapter 2

IN MY IDEAL GARDEN I WOULD WANT GRASSY PATHWAYS BORDERED BY LUSH BEDS OF FLOWERS. *The garden would be filled with friendly creatures such as birds, a cat, a bunny, a turtle—even a naughty raccoon. Elegant stone balustrades would be covered with cascades of perfumed roses and the arch entries would brim over with wisteria.*

ENGLISH GARDEN PILLOW

FINISHED MEASUREMENTS

- 12 x 12 inches (31 x 31 cm)
- 144 stitches wide x 144 stitches high

MATERIALS

- 10 colors of Paternayan wool
- 12-mesh cotton canvas 16 x 16 inches (41 x 41 cm)
- Size 18 tapestry needle
- Finishing accessories: twisted cord, zipper, backing fabric, pillow form

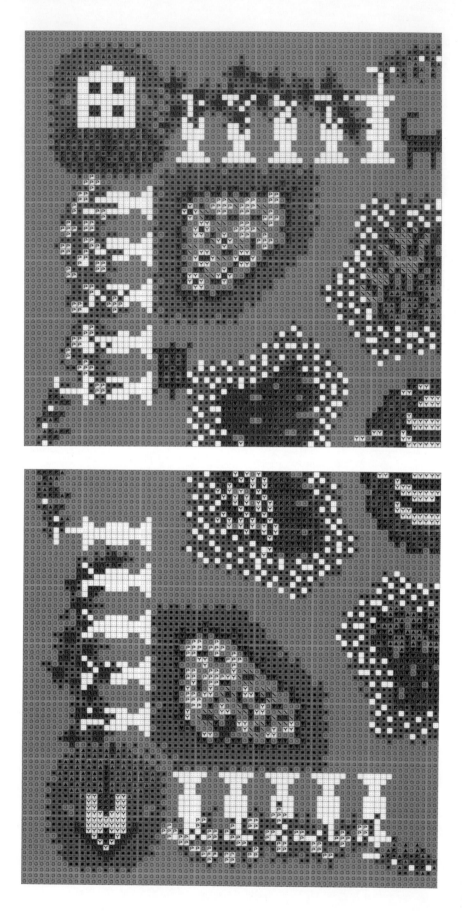

WORKING THE DESIGN

Use continental stitch throughout with 2 strands of Paternayan wool in your needle. To make the 'pupil' in the racoon's eye, stitch 1 small, green french knot in the middle of the 3 purple stitches that form the eye. Stitch 1 yellow french knot in the middle of the robin's head to create its eye. Use 1 strand for the French knots.

FINISHING

Trim the edges of the canvas to within 1 inch (2.5 cm) of the needlepoint stitches. Choose the color of your backing fabric carefully—you do not want it to overwhelm the needlepoint. If you are in doubt, find a color that matches the background color of your needlepoint. Using a piece of the backing fabric cut to the same size as the trimmed needlepoint, place back and front pieces with right sides together and stitch between the first and second row of needlepoint stitches, leaving an opening on one side for inserting the pillow filling. Turn the pillow right side out, insert the pillow filling, turn the edges of the opening, and slip stitch together (or put in a zipper). If desired, sew twisted cord over the seam that joins the pillow to the backing fabric.

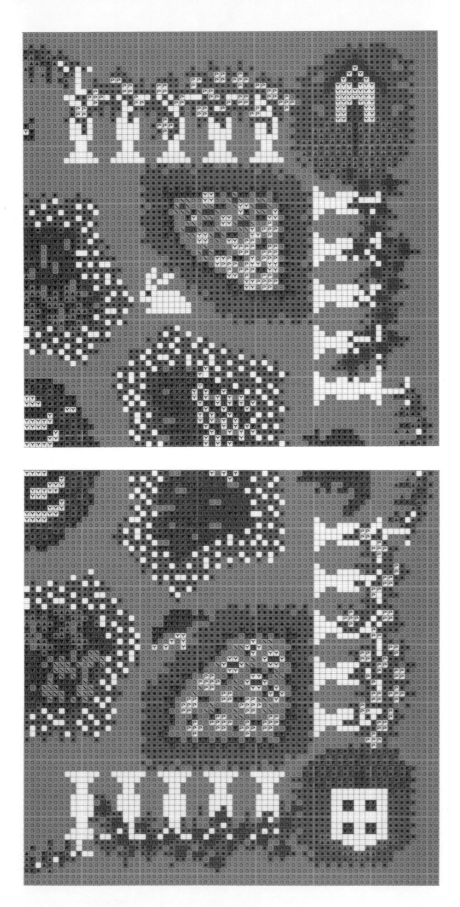

English Garden Pillow

PATERNAYAN PERSIAN WOOLS

Symbol	№	Color	Yards	Meters
◣	853	Orange	9	8
▼	480	Brown	18	16
▲	341	Lavender	9	8
◤	330	Dark Purple	9	8
G	630	Grass Green (BKGD)	60	55
R	950	Red	9	8
∷	948	Palest Pink	30	27
Y	726	Yellow	9	8
P	945	Pink	9	8
■	661	Dark Green	50	46

DESIGNER TIP

This is a perfect design to use for experimenting with fibers. Try overstitching the flowers with ribbon embroidery or stitch the flowers in shiny fibers such as silk, pearl cotton, or floss. You could stitch the animals in fuzzy-textured fibers. To make the grass softer and more heathery, use two very close shades of green wool at the same time in your needle.

DESIGNING ROSES WAS A REAL CHALLENGE FOR ME!

Realistic color shading was not something I had done much of so I had to keep trying. For weeks I tortured myself (and my family) as I stitched 45 prototypes in different sizes and colors. Out of those, I found four roses I liked, and I repeated them in this design. The moral of the story is to keep trying until you create something you are happy with.

RING
OF ROSES
PILLOW

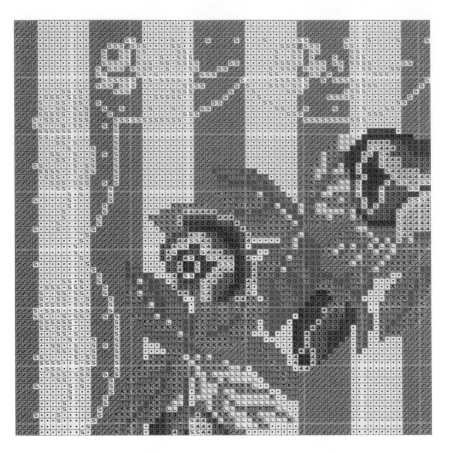

FINISHED MEASUREMENTS

- 12 x 12 inches (30.5 x 30.5 cm)
- 144 stitches wide x 144 stitches high

MATERIALS

- 11 colors of Paternayan wool
- 12-mesh cotton canvas 16 x 16 inches (41 x 41 cm)
- Size 18 tapestry needle
- Finishing accessories: twisted cord, zipper, backing fabric, pillow form

WORKING THE DESIGN

Use continental stitch throughout with 2 strands of Paternayan wool in your needle.

FINISHING

Trim the edges of the canvas to within 1 inch (2.5 cm) of the needlepoint stitches. Choose the color of your backing fabric carefully—you do not want it to overwhelm the needlepoint. If you are in doubt, find a color that matches the background color of your needlepoint. Using a piece of the backing fabric cut to the same size as the trimmed needlepoint, place back and front pieces with right sides together and stitch between the first and second row of needlepoint stitches, leaving an opening on one side for inserting the pillow filling. Turn the pillow right side out, insert the pillow filling, turn the edges of the opening, and slip stitch together (or put in a zipper). If desired, sew twisted cord over the seam that joins the pillow to the backing fabric.

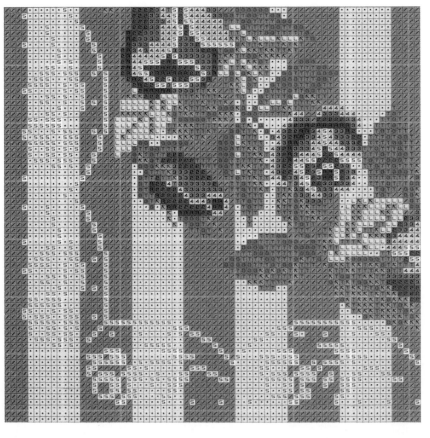

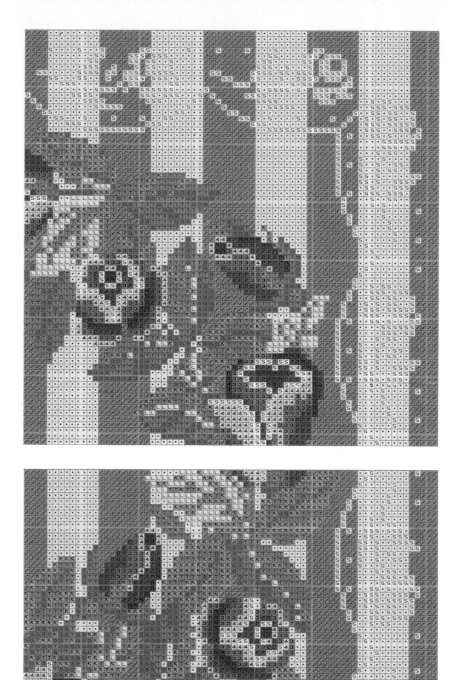

Ring of Roses Pillow

PATERNAYAN PERSIAN WOOLS

Symbol	№	Color	Yards	Meters
4	934	Pale Rose	9	8
3	932	Light Rose	9	8
5	935	Very Pale Rose	30	27
L	604	Light Hunter Green	18	16
T	521	Spruce Green	30	27
↖	602	Dark Hunter Green	18	16
R	930	Dark Rose	9	8
•	515	Light Blue (BKGD)	50	46
/	513	Med. Blue (BKGD)	50	46
2	931	Med. Rose	9	8
G	530	Dark Spruce Green	18	16

DESIGNER TIP

The roses would look very dramatic if you stitched the background in black and charcoal stripes or in two shades of navy blue.

THIS IS A REALLY FAST AND EASY PROJECT, and the cheerful pansy faces are a glad reminder of spring. For a more dramatic version you could stitch the background in dark green or black.

PANSY PINCUSHION

FINISHED MEASUREMENTS

- 3¾ inches (9.5 cm) in diameter
- 45 stitches in diameter

MATERIALS

- 16 colors of Paternayan wool
- 12-mesh cotton canvas 6 x 6 inches (15 x 15 cm)
- Size 18 tapestry needle
- Finishing accessories: pincushion base (see supplier list on page 124)

WORKING THE DESIGN

Use continental stitch throughout with 2 strands of Paternayan wool in your needle.

FINISHING

I used Creative Furnishings 3½-inch (9 cm) pincushion base. You could also use Sudberry Houses' 4½-inch (11 cm) pincushion base if you added 5 to 6 extra stitched rows to the outside edge of the pincushion design.

On the underside of the rounded top, measure and mark the center point on all four sides. Lay the needlepoint canvas over the rounded top, matching the center points of your needlepoint canvas to the center marks on the underside of the rounded top so that the needlepoint equally covers the top and extends a little bit under the underside. Staple gun or nail all four center points. Then, working from the center, attach the needlepoint so that it is evenly stretched over the top and sides of the rounded top. Gently press the covered top so that it slides into the opening of the pincushion base. Attach the top to the base with the screw provided. If the screw is too short, you may need to buy a longer one in order to securely hold the top to the base.

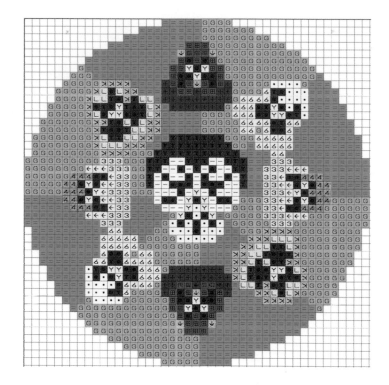

Pansy Pincushion

Symbol	No	Color		Yards	Meters
—	716	Palest Yellow		2	2
3	815	Palest Orange		2	2
4	812	Dark Orange		2	2
Y	772	Dark Yellow		2	2
6	713	Medium Yellow		2	2
■	320	Dark Plum		5	5
■	330	Purple		3	3
⊁	333	Medium Lavender		2	2
L	334	Pale Lavender		2	2
✢	850	Dark Spice		2	2
⊞	852	Medium Spice		2	2
↓	853	Light Spice		2	2
←	813	Medium Orange		2	2
=	630	Dark Green	(BKGD)	8	7
G	631	Light Green	(BKGD)	8	7
•	714	Light Yellow		2	2

PATERNAYAN PERSIAN WOOLS

DESIGNER TIP

To make this design fit a 4½-inch (11.5 cm) pincushion base, you will need to add 5 to 6 stitches around the entire outside border.

FEW FLOWERS MAKE ME AS HAPPY AS PARROT **TULIPS!** *I stitched the tulips with blue backgrounds as coasters for summer drinks and the ones with black backgrounds as dramatic winter coasters, perfect for my favorite mug of tea. They are stitched on plastic canvas—a great medium for coasters because it will not rot when it gets wet and never needs to be blocked or reblocked.*

TULIP COASTERS

FINISHED MEASUREMENTS
- 4 x 4 inches (10 x 10 cm)
- 56 stitches wide x 56 stitches high

MATERIALS
- 6 to 7 colors of Paternayan wool
- 14-mesh plastic canvas 5 x 5 inches (13 x 13 cm)
- Size 22 tapestry needle
- Finishing accessories: felt or synthetic suede, cork, ½-inch or ⅝-inch thick (1.3 cm or 1.5 cm) cording

WORKING THE DESIGN
Use continental stitch throughout with 1 strand of Paternayan wool in your needle.

TULIP COASTERS

FINISHING

Here's how to glue on the cork and give the coasters a finished look: Cut the cork 1 inch (2.5 cm) smaller than the coasters, and glue the cork to the back of the needlepoint so that each side of the cork is inset ½ inch (1.3 cm) from the outside edge of the needlepoint. Find ½- or ⅝-inch-thick (1.3 or 1.5 cm) cording that matches the background color and glue it so that it fills the ½-inch (1.3 cm) gap. This makes a nice finished border and covers the edges of the cork.

DESIGNER TIP

It's a good idea to glue a thin backing of cork to the bottom of the coasters. That way, if a drinks glass sweats (or spills), the water will not seep through the needlepoint and stain your tabletop.

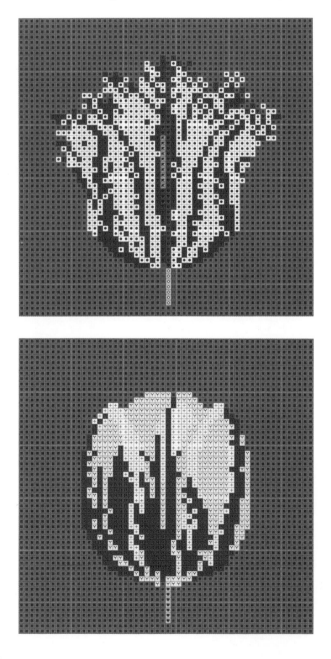

Red and White Tulip

Symbol	№	Color	Yards	Meters
K	942	Light Red	2	2
	941	Med. Red	4	4
◇	621	Med. Green	2	2
●	327	Palest Pink	5	5
H	620	Dark Green	2	2
	940	Dark Red	6	6
	543	Blue (BKGD)		
or	*220*	*Black*	7	6

PATERNAYAN PERSIAN WOOLS

Yellow and Red Tulip

PATERNAYAN PERSIAN WOOL

Symbol	№	Color	Yards	Meters
♥	621	Med. Green	2	2
+	772	Light Yellow	3	3
●	620	Dark Green	2	2
R	940	Dark Red	6	6
Y	771	Dark Yellow	4	4
	543	Blue (BKGD)		
or	*220*	*Black*	7	6

BY CHANGING THE BACKGROUND COLORS *on these magnets, I completely altered how the design looks. The way we see colors is affected by the colors they are paired with, and if you change one color, you alter the whole relationship. I encourage you to experiment with color. Consider stitching the background of these magnets with your favorite colors. To be sure you will like the end result, first stitch a small swatch to see how the colors look together before you stitch the entire design.*

CHERRY & LEMON MAGNETS

MATERIALS

- 5 to 7 colors of Paternayan wool
- 14-mesh plastic canvas 4 x 4 inches (10 x 10 cm)
- Size 22 tapestry needle
- Finishing accessories: felt or synthetic suede, 1-inch (2.5 cm) round or square magnets

WORKING THE DESIGN

Use continental stitch throughout with 1 strand of Paternayan wool in your needle. Leave the outside row unstitched. Finishing instructions are on page 67.

CHERRY MAGNET

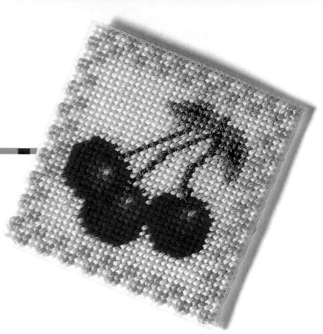

FINISHED MEASUREMENTS

- 2¾ x 2⅞ inches (7 x 7.3 cm)
- 38 stitches wide x 40 stitches high, including unstitched border

Cherry Magnet

PATERNAYAN PERSIAN WOOLS

Symbol	№	Color	Yards	Meters
W	260	White (BKGD)	5	5
●	770	Dark Yellow	3	3
–	810	Orange	1	1
X	852	Med Orange	1	1
R	970	Red	2	2
H	630	Dark Green	1	1
T	632	Light Green	1	1
U		Leave unstitched		

ALTERNATIVE BACKGROUND COLORS

W	220	Black	5	5
W	550	Blue	5	5
W	853	Dark Orange	5	5

DESIGNER TIP

To make the cherries and lemons look smooth and shiny the way they do in real life, try stitching them in silk or pearl cotton.

LEMON MAGNET

FINISHED MEASUREMENTS

- 2⅓ x 2¾ inches (6.3 x 7 cm)
- 38 stitches wide x 32 stitches high, including unstitched border

Lemon Magnet

PATERNAYAN PERSIAN WOOLS

Symbol	№	Color	Yards	Meters
W	260	White (BKGD)	4	4
+	772	Light Yellow	3	3
●	770	Dark Yellow	3	3
H	630	Dark Green	2	2
—	810	Orange	3	3
U		Leave unstitched		

ALTERNATIVE BACKGROUND COLORS

W	220	Black	4	4
W	331	Purple	4	4
W	940	Red	4	4

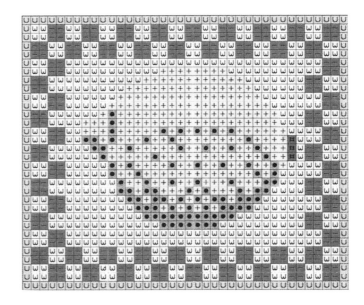

FINISHING ALL THE MAGNETS

You can leave the backs unfinished or you can finish them by gluing a piece of felt or synthetic suede (trimmed so that it is slightly smaller than the magnet) to the back of the stitched piece. Then glue a 1-inch (2.5 cm) round or square magnet to the back center of the needlepoint and allow it to completely dry before using.

HISTORICALLY, CRAZY-QUILT DESIGNS OFTEN FEATURED FABRIC PATCHES *with embroidered designs surrounded by decoratively stitched borders. I used high Victorian colors typical of the period—olive green, eggplant purple, mauve, and mustard yellow. To translate this into needlepoint I stitched favorite subjects in the center of each patch. Then I topstitched the borders of the patches with herringbone, featherstitch, cross-stitch, and French knots to make the needlepoint really look like a crazy quilt.*

CRAZY QUILT PILLOW & FOOTSTOOL

FINISHED MEASUREMENTS

- 10 x 10 inches (25 x 25 cm)
- 120 stitches wide x 120 stitches high

MATERIALS

- 11 colors of Paternayan wool
- 12-mesh cotton canvas 14 x 14 inches (36 x 36 cm)
- Size 18 tapestry needle
- Finishing accessories: FOR PILLOW— twisted cord, zipper, backing fabric, pillow form. FOR FOOTSTOOL—stuffing; stool, which can be ordered from Mark Arnold or Creative Furnishings. See supplier list on page 124.

WORKING THE DESIGN

Use continental stitch throughout with 2 strands of Paternayan wool in your needle.

FINISHING THE PILLOW

Trim the edges of the canvas to within 1 inch (2.5 cm) of the needlepoint stitches. Choose the color of your backing fabric carefully—you do not want it to overwhelm the needlepoint. If you are in doubt, find a color that matches the background color of your needlepoint. Using a piece of the backing fabric cut to the same size as the trimmed needlepoint, place back and front pieces with right sides together and stitch between the first and second row of needlepoint stitches, leaving an opening on one side for inserting the pillow filling. Turn the pillow right side out, insert the pillow filling, turn the edges of the opening, and slip stitch together (or put in a zipper). If desired, sew twisted cord over the seam that joins the pillow to the backing fabric.

FINISHING THE FOOTSTOOL

On the underside of the wooden top piece, measure and mark the center points of all four sides. Lay the needlepoint canvas over the wooden top, matching the center points of your needlepoint canvas to the center marks on the underside of the wooden top. The stitched needlepoint should equally cover the top and sides of the wooden base, allowing some slack for the stuffing. Staple or nail three sides of the wooden top piece. Evenly fill the space between the needlepoint and the wood with batting to make a nicely rounded top, then staple the remaining open side so that the entire needlepoint is attached to the wooden top. Gently press the padded top so that it slides into the opening of the footstool base.

DESIGNER TIP

If you feel creative, you can use the shapes of my patches as your design template and design a few personalized images of favorite things in your life to fill in the patches. This way you can create a commemorative crazy quilt for yourself or as a gift. This design lends itself perfectly to embellishment with silk ribbon and beads.

Crazy Quilt Pillow & Footstool

PATERNAYAN PERSIAN WOOLS

Symbol	№	Color	Yards	Meters	Symbol	№	Color	Yards	Meters
⊐	321	Med. Plum	18	16	◇	327	Palest Pink	18	16
Ⓘ	303	Lavender	18	16	●	902	Rose Red	18	16
▼	880	Ginger Brown	18	16	H	544	Sky Blue	18	16
▲	772	Bright Yellow	18	16	T	725	Autumn Yellow	18	16
◤	320	Dark Plum	18	16	■	501	Dark Blue	18	16
♥	652	Olive Green	18	16					

■ I BASED THESE PROJECTS
■ ON TWO CLASSIC AMISH
QUILT DESIGNS *and did them
originally as refrigerator magnets. The star rug
(10-mesh plastic canvas) and the star pillows
(14-mesh plastic canvas) are all stitched from
the same chart to illustrate how you can alter
a design simply by using different sizes of
needlepoint canvas. I stitched the star design
all in metallics as a Christmas tree ornament
and then realized it would make a nice
brooch, as well.*

AMISH QUILT
SQUARES

FINISHED
MEASUREMENTS

- 2 x 2 inches (5 x 5 cm)
- 31 stitches wide x 31
stitches high

MATERIALS

- 3 or 4 colors of Paternayan wool
- 14-mesh plastic canvas
3 x 3 inches (8 x 8 cm)
- Size 22 tapestry needle
- Finishing accessories: felt or
synthetic suede, 1-inch (2.5 cm)
round or square magnets

WORKING THE DESIGN

Use continental stitch throughout with 1 strand
of Paternayan wool in your needle. For the
Christmas version (photo on page 89), use
2 strands of Madeira 'Glamour' Metallics.

FINISHING

You can leave the backs unfinished or you can
finish them by gluing a piece of felt or synthetic
suede (trimmed so that it is slightly smaller than
the magnet) to the back of the stitched piece.
Then glue a 1-inch (2.5 cm) round or square
magnet to the back center of the needlepoint
and allow it to completely dry before using.

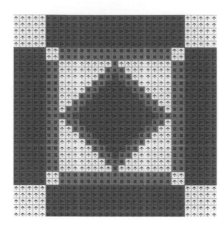

Amish Star Pattern

Symbol	№	Color	Yards	Meters
↑	771	Yellow	2	2
■	541	Blue	2	2
▶	970	Red	2	2
⊞	696	Green	2	2

PATERNAYAN PERSIAN WOOL

ALTERNATIVE COLORWAYS

PATERNAYAN PERSIAN WOOL

↑	970	Red	2	2
■	696	Green	2	2
▶	771	Yellow	2	2
⊞	541	Blue	2	2

PATERNAYAN PERSIAN WOOL

↑	971	Red	2	2
■	540	Dark Blue	2	2
▶	543	Light Blue	2	2
⊞	521	Sea Green	2	2

ANCHOR EMBROIDERY FLOSS

↑	128	Palest Blue	2	2
■	139	Dark Blue	2	2
▶	131	Med. Blue	2	2
⊞	130	Light Blue	2	2

MADEIRA METALLIC 'GLAMOUR'

↑	2425	Gold	1 spool
■	2438	Blue	1 spool
▶	2414	Red	1 spool
⊞	2458	Green	1 spool

DESIGNER TIPS

Sew fabric to the backs of the little seat covers and they will become perfect dollhouse pillows. You could also sew them to a ribbon to make a vertical wall hanging (see the green cats on page 43).

Use metallic thread to transform the Amish design into a glittering brooch (below) or a Christmas ornament (page 89).

Amish Diamond Pattern

PATERNAYAN PERSIAN WOOL

Symbol	№	Color	Yards	Meters
↑	771	Yellow	2	2
■	541	Blue	2	2
▶	970	Red	2	2

ALTERNATIVE COLORWAYS

PATERNAYAN PERSIAN WOOL

↑	971	Red	2	2
■	521	Sea Green	2	2
▶	543	Light Blue	2	2

PATERNAYAN PERSIAN WOOL

↑	543	Light Blue	2	2
■	521	Sea Green	2	2
▶	971	Red	2	2

PATERNAYAN PERSIAN WOOL

↑	541	Dark Blue	2	2
■	696	Green	2	2
▶	970	Red	2	2

MADEIRA METALLIC 'GLAMOUR'

↑	2425	Gold	1 spool
■	2438	Blue	1 spool
▶	2414	Red	1 spool

ORIENTAL EARRING HOLDER

▮ HAD SEEN AN EARRING HOLDER FRAME THAT WAS MADE OUT OF WINDOW SCREEN MESH *and I immediately wanted one for myself. While looking at it, I realized with surprise that needlepoint canvas was a perfect substitute for screen mesh. I went to my local art supply store and bought a set of stretcher bars like those used to stretch a small canvas for a painting. Then I stitched a design to fit the frame's outside border but left the inside area unstitched. My design was borrowed from the border of an oriental carpet in my living room.*

FINISHED MEASUREMENTS

- 9 x 11½ inches (23 x 29 cm)
- 116 stitches wide x 147 stitches high

MATERIALS

- 15 colors of Paternayan wool
- 13-mesh cotton canvas 13 x 15½ inches (33 x 39.5 cm)
- Size 18 tapestry needle
- Finishing accessories: two 10-inch and two 8-inch stretcher bars

WORKING THE DESIGN

Use continental stitch throughout with 2 strands of Paternayan wool in your needle.

FINISHING

Staple or nail the finished blocked needlepoint so that 4 red and white stitched rows wrap around and extend over the narrow sides of the stretcher bars and the needlepoint is stretched tautly.

DESIGNER TIP

You can use the dimensions of this earring holder frame to create your own border pattern (or adapt another design in this book for that purpose). The best way is to chart your design on graph paper first, then adjust the dimensions of the border before you begin stitching so that you know it will fit the frame dimensions.

Oriental Earring Holder

PATERNAYAN PERSIAN WOOLS

Symbol	№	Color	Yards	Meters
ר	221	Charcoal	8	8
—	262	Cream	25	23
I	480	Terracotta	8	8
1	420	Dark Brown	8	8
O	832	Orange	8	8
/	725	Dark Yellow	8	8
Y	734	Light Yellow	8	8
8	570	Navy Blue	15	14
■	540	Cobalt Blue	10	9
+	970	Bright Red	15	14
R	840	Medium Red	25	23
↓	900	Dark Red	8	8
←	930	Light Red	15	14
▽	530	Dark Green	8	8
G	532	Medium Green	8	8

THIS IS A FRAGMENT OF A TURKISH KAZAK RUG DESIGN *that I return to again and again. I've discovered that having a nice checkbook cover really does make paying bills a bit less painful! You can use this design to make yourself a matching eyeglasses case.*

KAZAK CHECKBOOK COVER

FINISHED MEASUREMENTS

- 7¼ x 8¼ inches (18.5 x 21.5 cm)
- 87 stitches wide x 99 stitches high

MATERIALS

- 11 colors of Paternayan wool
- 12-mesh cotton canvas 12 x 13 inches (31 x 33.5 cm)
- Size 18 tapestry needle
- Finishing accessories: backing fabric

WORKING THE DESIGN

Use continental stitch throughout with 2 strands of Paternayan wool in your needle.

FINISHING

Cut away the excess canvas, leaving ½ inch (1.3 cm) of unstitched canvas for turning. Cut one piece of lining fabric for the checkbook lining, 8¾ inches high by 7½ inches wide (22.5 x 19 cm), and two pieces of lining fabric, 7½ inches wide by 7½ inches high (19 x 19 cm) for the pockets. Fold the pocket pieces in half and baste them to each end of the lining so that the folded edges of the pockets face one another. With right sides together, pin or tack the needlepoint to the lining and machine stitch all around, leaving a 4-inch (10 cm) opening on one side. To avoid having any unstitched needlepoint canvas showing, you can machine stitch along the space between the first and second row of the stitched needlepoint. Trim turnings away from the corners and turn to the right side. Slip stitch the opening together.

Kazak Checkbook Cover

Symbol	№	PATERNAYAN PERSIAN WOOLS Color	Yards	Meters
−	260	White (BKGD)	22	20
	420	Dark Coffee Brown	16	15
5	734	Light Honey Gold	12	11
6	725	Autumn Yellow	9	8
8	571	Light Navy Blue	9	8
9	570	Dark Navy Blue	12	11
/	530	Dark Spruce Green	6	6
\	532	Spruce Green	6	6
₪	900	Dark Burgundy Red	12	11
⊞	930	Med. Brick Red	8	7
↓	968	Bright Red	18	17

DESIGNER TIP

If you mix cream- and white-colored wool together in your needle, the white background will take on a more antique look. It's best to use a stiff fabric for the inside finishing of the checkbook.

■ NSPIRED BY THE COLORS AND
  ■ IMAGES OF THE SOUTHWEST, *I combined*
pairs of whiptail lizards and rattlesnakes with miniature Navajo
rug patterns. I mixed two colors of dusty pink to create the heathery
background for the lizards and snakes. This piece is stitched on plastic
canvas so that no blocking is required. Each individual rug design
could be stitched on its own as a handsome dollhouse rug.

SOUTHWEST
MIRROR FRAME

FINISHED MEASUREMENTS
- 3¾ x 3¾ inches (9.5 x 9.5 cm)
- 107 stitches square

MATERIALS
- 14 colors of Paternayan wool and 1 color Kreinik Metallic
- 10-mesh plastic canvas 10¾ x 12 inches (28 x 31 cm)
- Size 18 tapestry needle
- Finishing accessories: see Finishing instructions below

WORKING THE DESIGN
Use continental stitch throughout with 2 strands of Paternayan wool
and 1 strand of Kreinik.

FINISHING
Attach a mirror to the back of needlepoint. Back the mirror with a thin
piece of wood and securely attach a wire for hanging, or have the mirror professionally backed and finished with a mirror.

DESIGNER TIP

*If you prefer to stitch this on
cotton canvas, you could have
a mirror cut to the exact inside
dimensions of the frame, and
glue the mirror onto the blank
needlepoint canvas. A picture
could be substituted in place
of the mirror. As an added
finishing touch, you could sew
on brush fringe, or have the
mirror framed with wood that
complements your home's decor.*

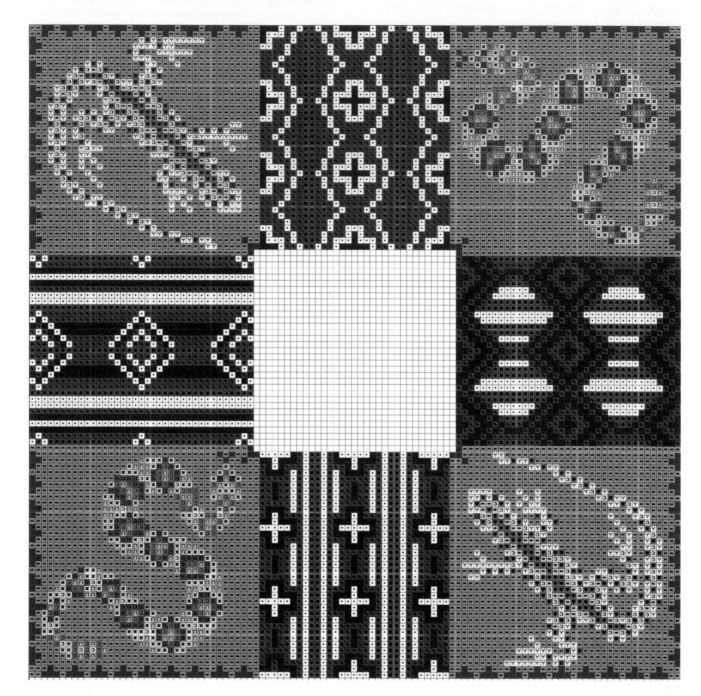

Southwest Mirror Frame

PATERNAYAN PERSIAN WOOLS

Symbol	№	Color	Yards	Meters		Symbol	№	Color	Yards	Meters		Symbol	№	Color	Yards	Meters
♥	221	Charcoal	5	5		◧	471	Dark Toast	5	5		▬	873	Pale Rust (BKGD)	25	23
•	756	Pale Yellow	15	14		Ⅲ	472	Medium Toast	5	5			872	Rust (BKGD)	25	23
▣	220	Black	15	14		⊓	473	Light Toast	7	6						
3	754	Medium Gold	6	6		✳	474	Pale Toast	9	8						
	570	Navy Blue	15	14		▬	753	Dark Gold	4	4						
◪	930	Rusty Rose	20	18		Y	755	Light Gold	10	9						

Note: Use 1 ply each of #873 and #872 together in your needle to create the mixed background color.

KREINIK MEDIUM #16 BRAID

Symbol	№	Color		
G	060	Dark Pewter		1 Spool

SPECIAL OCCASIONS

Chapter 3

**I COLLECT SANTAS—
THE MORE UNUSUAL
THE BETTER.** *I think Santa must be
an animal lover so I included a dog who looks
like my white shepherd, Bella, some cats, and a
bird to keep him company. This design can also
be finished as a trivet or a small pillow.*

SANTA & FRIENDS TRAY OR CHRISTMAS ORNAMENT

FINISHED TRAY MEASUREMENTS
- 7 x 7 inches (18 x 18 cm)
- 49 stitches wide x 49 stitches high

FINISHED ORNAMENT MEASUREMENTS
- 3½ x 3½ inches (9 cm x 9 cm)
  (See photograph on page 89.)

SANTA & FRIENDS TRAY
OR CHRISTMAS ORNAMENT

MATERIALS

- 9 colors of Paternayan wool plus gold metallic
- Tray: 7-mesh cotton canvas 11 x 11 inches (28 x 28 cm)
- Ornament: 14-mesh plastic canvas 5 x 5 inches (13 x 13 cm)
- Size 18 tapestry needle (for 7-mesh canvas)
- Size 22 tapestry needle (for 14-mesh canvas)
- Finishing accessories: FOR TRAY—see supplier list on page 124; FOR ORNAMENT BACKING—synthetic suede

WORKING THE DESIGN

Use continental stitch throughout with 4 strands of Paternayan wool for the tray on 7-mesh canvas, and 1 strand of Paternayan wool for the Christmas ornament on 14-mesh canvas. Use 5 strands of Madeira 'Glamour' for the tray on 7-mesh canvas and 2 strands of Madeira 'Glamour' for the ornament on 14-mesh canvas. Stitch the outermost border of the ornament in red and green metallic threads.

FINISHING THE TRAY

I used Sudberry Houses' red 9-inch (23 cm) tray (see suppliers list on page 124) and had my framer cut a blue mat to make my 7-inch (18 cm) design fit the tray.

If you prefer, before you begin stitching, cut your needlepoint canvas to allow for a 5-inch (13 cm) border around the design. Then you could stitch an additional 1¼-inch (3.5 cm) needlepoint border around all sides of the design to make it fit the tray exactly.

FINISHING THE ORNAMENT

See the finishing instructions on page 93.

DESIGNER TIP

If you are stitching the design as a Christmas ornament, purchase 1/4 of the amounts given.

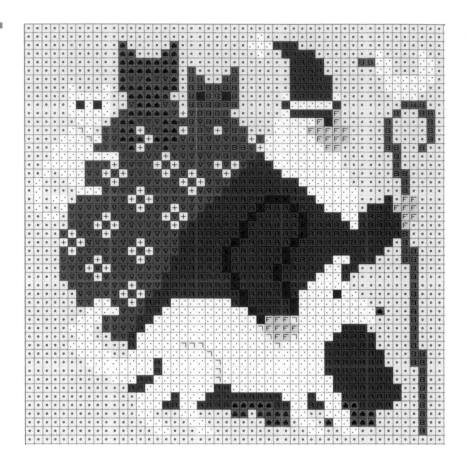

Santa & Friends Tray

PATERNAYAN PERSIAN WOOLS

Symbol	№	Color	Yards	Meters
▲	221	Charcoal	9	8
⌐	546	Sky Blue	10	9
·	260	White	28	26
B	720	Light Brown	20	18
•	771	Yellow (BKGD)	35	32
■	540	Cobalt Blue	10	9
F	490	Flesh	10	9
R	970	Red	23	21
▽	680	Green	20	18

MADEIRA METALLIC 'GLAMOUR'

+	2425	Gold Metallic	30	28

HOLIDAYS ARE A GREAT EXCUSE TO GO WILD WITH GLITTER AND METALLIC THREADS! *Needlepoint Christmas tree ornaments show up best when they include metallic thread and beads, because the ornaments reflect the trees lights. I stitched two versions of the sheep ornament—one using natural wool for the sheep with a metallic background, and the other using fuzzy metallics for the sheep, as well as for the background and border. There are so many different metallic threads in silk or floss, that it's a good idea to experiment to find combinations you like. For example, the sheep would look great with a background stitched in pearl cotton; to make the tree even more sparkly, you could use a metallic thread for the background instead of the floss I used here.*

CHRISTMAS ORNAMENTS

EWE WITH LAMB

FINISHED MEASUREMENTS

- 3¼ x 2¾ inches (8.5 x 7 cm)
- 32 stitches wide x 28 stitches high

MATERIALS

- 10 colors of various fibers
- 10-mesh plastic canvas 4 x 4 inches (10 x 10 cm)
- Size 18 tapestry needle
- Finishing accessories: felt or synthetic suede for backing

WORKING THE DESIGN

Use continental stitch throughout with 1 strand of Alpaca, patent leather, and all metallics in your needle. Use all 12 strands of Splendor silk in your needle.

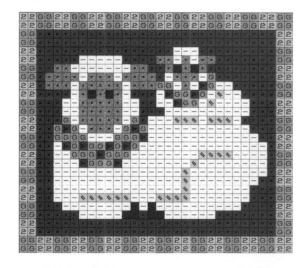

DESIGNER TIP

Beads and needlepoint are wonderful together. When making Christmas ornaments, the more beads—especially sparkling ones—the better. You can also sew shiny small buttons onto needlepoint. Many buttons depicting Christmas themes are available year-round.

Ewe with Lamb

Symbol	№	Color	Yards	Meters
RAINBOW GALLERY ALPACA 18				
•	AL64	Black	3	3
╲	AL61	Gray	2	2
—	AL52	Cream	2	2
RAINBOW GALLERY PATENT LEATHER				
■	PL1	Black	1	1
RAINBOW GALLERY SPLENDOR SILK				
■	S868	Blue	1	1
G	S829	Green	3	3
		or #258 Madeira Carat, Green Metallic		
▶	S821	Red	1	1
RAINBOW GALLERY GOLD RUSH #12				
2	DG6C	Gold Metallic	3	3
MADEIRA CARAT				
■	270	Red Metallic (BKGD)	4	4

SNOWFLAKE

FINISHED MEASUREMENTS

- 3 x 3 inches (8 x 8 cm)
- 41 stitches wide x 41 stitches high

MATERIALS

- 3 colors of various fibers
- 14-mesh plastic canvas 4 x 4 inches (10 x 10 cm)
- Size 22 tapestry needle
- Finishing accessories: felt or synthetic suede for backing
- Beads: 4 glass stars (6S-118AB) and 41 pearls (WP/3 mm) from A.K. Beads (see supplier list on page 124)

WORKING THE DESIGN

Use continental stitch throughout with 6 strands of DMC floss and 1 full strand (i.e. all the plies) of Kreinik and Madeira.

BEADING: After the entire design is stitched, sew 1 glass star onto each of the four corners. Sew 1 pearl to the center of the design and sew 10 pearls per side to the four outside edges of the ornament.

Snowflake

Symbol	№	Color	Amount
			DMC FLOSS
⠒	809	Ice Blue	2 skeins
			KREINIK MEDIUM #16 BRAID
◆	329	Blue/Purple Metallic	1 spool
			MADEIRA 'GLAMOUR'
—	2400	White Metallic	1 spool

CHRISTMAS TREE

FINISHED MEASUREMENTS

- 3 x 3½ inches (8 x 9 cm)
- 41 stitches wide x 49 stitches high, including unstitched border rows

MATERIALS

- 3 colors of Madeira Metallics and Floss
- 14-mesh plastic canvas 4 x 4½ inches (10 x 11 cm)
- Size 22 tapestry needle
- Finishing accessories: felt or synthetic suede for backing.
- Beads: 1 large gold star sequin ½ inch (1.3 cm); 13 small round sequins (1 cm); 12 star sequins (5 mm) in gold, red, blue, and silver; 25 gold seed beads; 17 white pearls (3 mm); and 20 inches (51 cm) red sequin trim

WORKING THE DESIGN

Use continental stitch throughout with 6 strands of Madeira floss and 1 full strand (i.e. all the plies) of Madeira 'Glamour'. and Madeira.

BEADING AND EMBELLISHMENT: After the entire design is stitched, sew on white pearl beads in the shape of a garland (see project photograph above). Decorate the rest of the tree with round and star sequins, sewing 1 gold seed bead onto the center of each sequin. Baste the red sequin trimming over the unstitched rows on all four sides around the tree. Sew the large gold star sequin to the top of the tree and sew 1 gold seed bead in the center of the large star sequin.

Tree

		MADEIRA 'GLAMOUR'				MADEIRA COTTON FLOSS		
Symbol	№	Color	Amount	Symbol	№	Color	Yards	Meters
G	2425	Gold Metallic	1 spool	W	0101	White	11	10
●	2458	Green Metallic	1 spool	U		Leave unstitched		

CHRISTMAS STOCKING

FINISHED MEASUREMENTS

- 3½ x 3¼ inches (9 x 8.5 cm)
- 49 stitches wide x 47 stitches high

MATERIALS:

- 4 colors of Kreinik Metallics
- 14-mesh plastic canvas 4½ x 4½ inches (11.5 x 11.5 cm)
- Size 22 tapestry needle
- Finishing accessories: felt or synthetic suede for backing
- Beads: 7 red glass heart beads (6 mm) from A.K. Beads (see supplier list on page 124)

WORKING THE DESIGN

Use continental stitch throughout with 1 full strand (i.e. all the plies) of Kreinik Metallic. Beading: After the entire design is stitched, sew 1 glass heart over each needlepoint heart.

FINISHING ALL THE ORNAMENTS

To finish the ornaments, sew a short length of dark green metallic (or other fiber) to the top left and right sides of the ornament to form a 1½-inch (4 cm) hanging loop. It's a good idea to use at least 2 full strands of the fiber to make a strong loop. Then glue a piece of felt or synthetic suede (trimmed so that the backing does not show from the front) to the back of the stitched piece.

Christmas Stocking

KREINIK 1/16TH RIBBON

Symbol	№	Color	Amount
−	032	White	1 spool
■	051HL	Blue	1 spool
▶	003HL	Red	1 spool
G	008	Green	1 spool

I BELIEVE THAT ANGELS MUST
EXIST IN ALL COLORS *so I stitched*
them that way: an African angel in a dashiki, a
Scandinavian angel in Nordic dress, a Native American
angel in Southwest dress, and an Asian angel in a kimono.

ETHNIC ANGELS

FINISHED MEASUREMENTS

- 4 x 4 inches (10 x 10 cm)
- 40 stitches wide x 40 stitches high

MATERIALS

- 6 to 8 colors of Paternayan wool plus gold metallic
- 10-mesh plastic canvas 5 x 5 inches (13 x 13 cm)
- Size 18 tapestry needle
- Finishing accessories: framing materials, felt or synthetic suede as backing for coasters

WORKING THE DESIGN

Use continental stitch throughout with 2 strands of Paternayan wool and 1 strand of Rainbow Gallery Gold Rush #12.

FINISHING

I strongly advise you to have your needlepoint professionally framed using only acid-free materials.

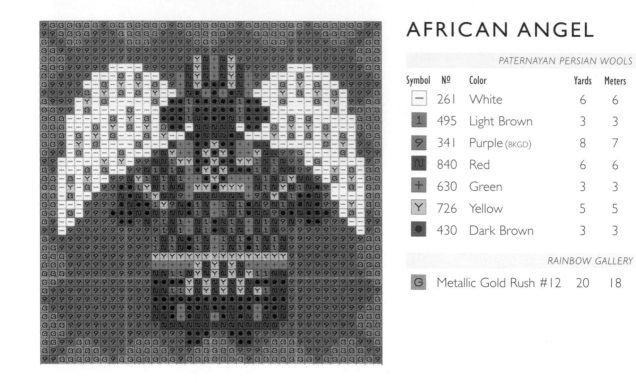

AFRICAN ANGEL

		PATERNAYAN PERSIAN WOOLS		
Symbol	№	Color	Yards	Meters
−	261	White	6	6
1	495	Light Brown	3	3
9	341	Purple (BKGD)	8	7
N	840	Red	6	6
+	630	Green	3	3
Y	726	Yellow	5	5
●	430	Dark Brown	3	3
		RAINBOW GALLERY		
G		Metallic Gold Rush #12	20	18

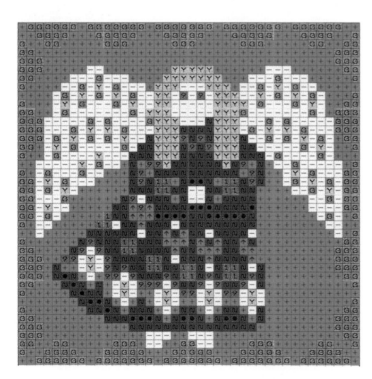

SCANDINAVIAN ANGEL

		PATERNAYAN PERSIAN WOOLS		
Symbol	№	Color	Yards	Meters
−	261	White	6	6
1	495	Light Brown	2	2
9	341	Purple	2	2
↑	591	Turquoise	2	2
N	840	Red	7	6
+	630	Green (BKGD)	8	7
Y	726	Yellow	5	5
●	430	Dark Brown	2	2
		RAINBOW GALLERY		
G		Metallic Gold Rush #12	20	18

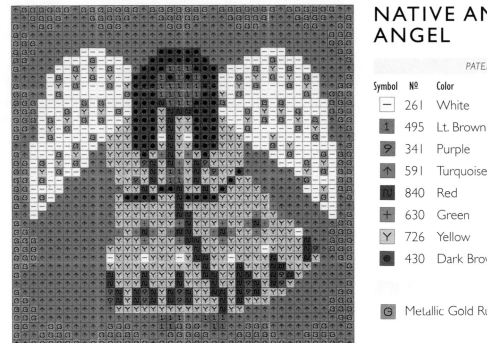

NATIVE AMERICAN ANGEL

PATERNAYAN PERSIAN WOOLS

Symbol	Nº	Color	Yards	Meters
−	261	White	5	5
1	495	Lt. Brown	2	2
9	341	Purple	2	2
↑	591	Turquoise (BKGD)	8	7
Ω	840	Red	3	3
+	630	Green	2	2
Y	726	Yellow	6	6
●	430	Dark Brown	3	3

RAINBOW GALLERY

G	Metallic Gold Rush #12		20	18

ASIAN ANGEL

PATERNAYAN PERSIAN WOOLS

Symbol	Nº	Color	Yards	Meters
−	261	White	6	6
9	341	Purple	5	5
↑	591	Turquoise	5	5
Ω	840	Red (BKGD)	8	7
Y	726	Yellow	5	2
●	430	Dark Brown	2	2

RAINBOW GALLERY

G	Metallic Gold Rush #12		20	18

DESIGNER TIP

These angel designs are just the right size to use as coasters. Or, stitch them on 14-mesh canvas to create charming little Christmas tree ornaments.

HERE IS A DESIGN NOT IN MY USUAL REPERTOIRE—IT WAS A CHALLENGE, AND I THINK THE END RESULT IS NOT BAD FOR A "SHIKSA"! *I tried to stretch myself creatively, which was fun. My editor, Deborah, taught me what Hanukkah was all about. I thought the dreidels were so much fun that I surrounded the menorah with lots of them.*

HANUKKAH WALL HANGING

FINISHED MEASUREMENTS
- 9¾ x 9¾ inches (25 x 25 cm)
- 97 stitches wide x 97 stitches high

MATERIALS:
- 22 colors of various fibers
- 10-mesh cotton canvas 14 x 14 inches (36 x 36 cm)
- Size 18 tapestry needle
- Finishing accessories: two ¼-inch (1 cm) dowels, 4 wooden Star of Davids (optional) and eight ½-inch (1.3 cm) gold 'coins'

WORKING THE DESIGN
Use continental stitch throughout with 3 strands of Paternayan wool, 2 strands of DMC pearl cotton #3, and 3 strands of Kreinik metallics. Use 5 strands DMC floss to stitch the characters on the dreidels.

Once the design is stitched and blocked, sew on the 'coins' as shown in the photograph.

FINISHING
Turn under the left and right sides of the needlepoint (so that the blank canvas does not show) and slip stitch them. Do the same for the top and bottom, leaving enough space to insert the ¼-inch (1 cm) dowels.

Cut four Stars of David out of ¾-inch-thick (2 cm) wood and drill a ¼-inch (1 cm) hole between two points of each star. Paint the stars on all sides with one coat of primer and several coats of bright gold paint. Let them dry thoroughly (it is a good idea to put a final coat of sealer over the paint to prevent the gold from rubbing off onto the needlepoint). Insert the dowel ends into the star holes and secure with glue. To make a hanger, tie clear fishing line (or a pretty ribbon) to the left and right sides of the top dowel in the space between the stars and the needlepoint.

DESIGNER TIP
You could sew little dreidels to the spaces between the wooden rods and the needlepoint.

PATERAYAN PERSIAN WOOL			
Symbol	№	Color	Amount
8	543	Blue (BKGD)	90 yds 82 m

MADIERA METALLIC #8			
Π	8013	Bright Gold	8 yds 7 m

DMC FLOSS			
	310	Black	1 skein
	(for letters on dreidels)		

DMC #3 PERLE COTON			
Symbol	№	Color	Amount
●	Blanc	White	1 skein
5	727	Light Yellow	1 skein
Y	743	Med Yellow	1 skein
⊞	797	Royal Blue	1 skein
4	3325	Pale Blue	1 skein
⊡	740	Orange	1 skein
⊞	349	Light Red	1 skein
⊞	498	Med Red	1 skein
⊠	669	Dark Green	1 skein
→	701	Light Green	1 skein

KREINIK MEDIUM #16 BRAID			
Symbol	№	Color	Amount
✳	001HL	Silver	1 spool
⊐	032C	White	1 spool
⊥	212	Light Gold	1 spool
▼	221	Gold	4 spools
▲	091	Pale Yellow	1 spool
◸	203	Red/Gold	1 spool
♥	085	Green	1 spool
◇	094	Sky Blue	1 spool
●	033	Dark Blue	1 spool
⊞	242HL	Purple	1 spool

FOR THIS VALENTINE FRAME I ALLOWED MYSELF TO GO TOTALLY OVER THE TOP. *How could I hold back when my real valentine (my husband, Jiri) is the man pictured inside the frame? This project uses a riot of colorful metallic threads mixed with silk, floss, and wool. I bet you didn't guess that this design was stitched on plastic canvas. It is a terrific medium for small projects which, because they are small, are difficult to block.*

VALENTINE FRAME

FINISHED MEASUREMENTS

- 8½ x 9¼ inches (22 x 24 cm)
- 119 stitches wide x 129 stitches high
- Inside dimensions—43 stitches wide x 63 stitches high

MATERIALS

- 24 colors of various fibers
- 14-mesh plastic canvas—1 sheet
- Size 22 tapestry needle

WORKING THE DESIGN

Use continental stitch throughout with 1 strand of Paternayan wool, 6 strands of DMC floss, and 1 strand of Kreinik metallics and silk.

FINISHING

I strongly advise you to have your needlepoint professionally framed using only acid-free materials. Have a framer back this and put a glass insert in the middle to protect the photograph.

DESIGNER TIP

If you want a tamer version of this design, use only wool. For a very dramatic, baroque look you could make the background black instead of white.

Valentine Frame

Symbol	№	Color	Amount
PATERNAYAN PERSIAN WOOLS			
═	841	Bright Red	4 yds 4 m
ℕ	900	Burgundy Red	4 yds 4 m
⧄	902	Dark Rose Red	4 yds 4 m
◈	969	Red	4 yds 4 m
⧄	940	Med. Red	4 yds 4 m
DMC FLOSS			
⋰	746	Cream (BKGRD)	8 skeins
•	Blanc	White	2 skeins
1	3806	Pink	1 skein
2	718	Pink	1 skein
3	3801	Pink	1 skein
4	321	Red	1 skein
6	3685	Dark Red	1 skein
KREINIK MEDIUM #16 BRAID			
△	332	Red/White	1 spool
⊟	007HL	Light Pink	1 spool
⊡	024	Deep Pink	1 spool
∥	024HL	Dark Pink	1 spool
↖	307	Red/Gold	1 spool
→	308	Red/Black	1 spool
↑	326	Red/Purple	1 spool
⊠	003C	Red	1 spool
G	221	Gold (BORDERS)	3 spools
KREINIK SILK SERICA			
I	1032	Pink	3 spools
⅃	1055	Deep Pink	1 spool
⊥	1114	Red	1 spool

■ **O**NE OF THE MANY REASONS I ADORED LIFE IN ITALY WAS BECAUSE EVERYWHERE YOU LOOKED THERE WERE CHERUBS. *Even my apartment was on Via Cherubini! This design would make a perfect gift for someone of the Gemini astrological sign or to celebrate the birth of twins. The small areas of purple help give the navy background depth, and the gold thread used to stitch the heart adds a touch of glamour.*

CHERUBS & STARS PILLOW

FINISHED MEASUREMENTS
- 15 x 12¾ inches (38 x 33 cm)
- 180 stitches wide x 154 stitches high

MATERIALS
- 8 colors of Paternayan wool plus gold metallic
- 12-mesh cotton canvas 19 x 17 inches (49 x 44 cm)
- Size 18 tapestry needle
- Finishing accessories: twisted cord, zipper, backing fabric, pillow form

WORKING THE DESIGN
Use continental stitch throughout with 2 strands of Paternayan wool and 4 strands of Madeira 'Glamour' in your needle.

FINISHING
Trim the edges of the canvas to within 1 inch (2.5 cm) of the needlepoint stitches. Choose the color of your backing fabric carefully—you do not want it to overwhelm the needlepoint. If you are in doubt, find a color that matches the background color of your needlepoint. Using a piece of the backing fabric cut to the same size as the trimmed needlepoint, place back and front pieces with right sides together and stitch between the first and second row of needlepoint stitches, leaving an opening on one side for inserting the pillow filling. Turn the pillow right side out, insert the pillow filling, turn the edges of the opening, and slip stitch together (or put in a zipper). If desired, sew twisted cord trim over the seam that joins the pillow to the backing fabric.

Cherubs & Stars Pillow

PATERNAYAN PERSIAN WOOLS

Symbol	Nº	Color	Yards	Meters
☒	846	Palest Orange	18	16
•	834	Light Orange	10	9
☉	833	Med. Orange	10	9
Y	772	Light Yellow	15	14
■	330	Purple	10	9
+	711	Dark Yellow	15	14
▪	571	Navy Blue (BKGD)	135	123
╲	832	Dark Orange	10	9

		MADEIRA METALLIC 'GLAMOUR'		
▼	2425	Gold Metallic	30	27

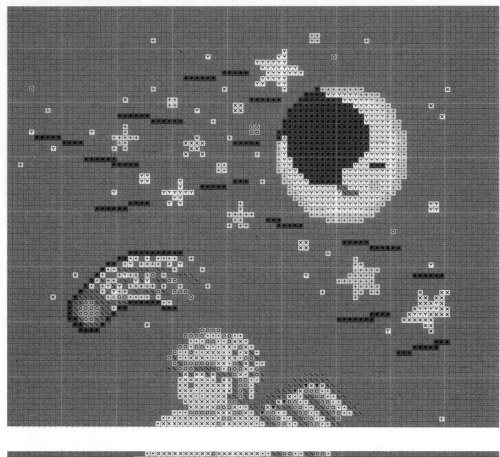

DESIGNER TIP

For added texture you could stitch the small stars in metallic threads, and the sun, moon, and comets in floss or silk.

THIS IS THE FIRST TIME I HAVE WORKED WITH A PASTEL COLOR PALETTE *and it was a revelation: the bunnies, chicks, eggs, and early flowers speak to us best in the fresh pastel colors of spring. The bunnies' tails are stitched with "Wisper" (see supplier information) which, when brushed, becomes fuzzy. The eggs are all stitched in silk so that they gleam against the floss background.*

EASTER NAPKIN RINGS

FINISHED MEASUREMENTS
- 7⅛ x 2½ inches (18.5 x 6.5 cm)
- 100 stitches wide x 37 stitches high

I KNOW IT WASN'T THE INTENTION OF OUR FOUNDING FATHERS, BUT THE AMERICAN FLAG IS A TERRIFICALLY DECORATIVE DESIGN, *particularly for summertime decor. I added the yellow ribbons because I stitched the design during the Gulf War when ribbons were one way of showing support for our military men and women.*

AMERICAN FLAG PILLOW

FINISHED MEASUREMENTS

- 16 x 13 inches (41 x 33.5 cm)
- 192 stitches wide x 157 stitches high

MATERIALS

- 5 colors of Paternayan wool
- 12-mesh cotton canvas 20 x 17 inches (51 x 44 cm)
- Size 18 tapestry needle
- Finishing accessories: twisted cord, zipper, backing fabric, pillow form

WORKING THE DESIGN

Use continental stitch throughout with 2 strands of Paternayan wool in your needle.

FINISHING

Trim the edges of the canvas to within 1 inch (2.5 cm) of the needlepoint stitches. Choose the color of your backing fabric carefully—you do not want it to overwhelm the needlepoint. If you are in doubt, find a color that matches the background color of your needlepoint. Using a piece of the backing fabric cut to the same size as the trimmed needlepoint, place back and front pieces with right sides together and stitch between the first and second row of needlepoint stitches, leaving an opening on one side for inserting the pillow filling. Turn the pillow right side out, insert the pillow filling, turn the edges of the opening, and slip stitch together (or put in a zipper). If desired, sew twisted cord trim over the seam that joins the pillow to the backing fabric.

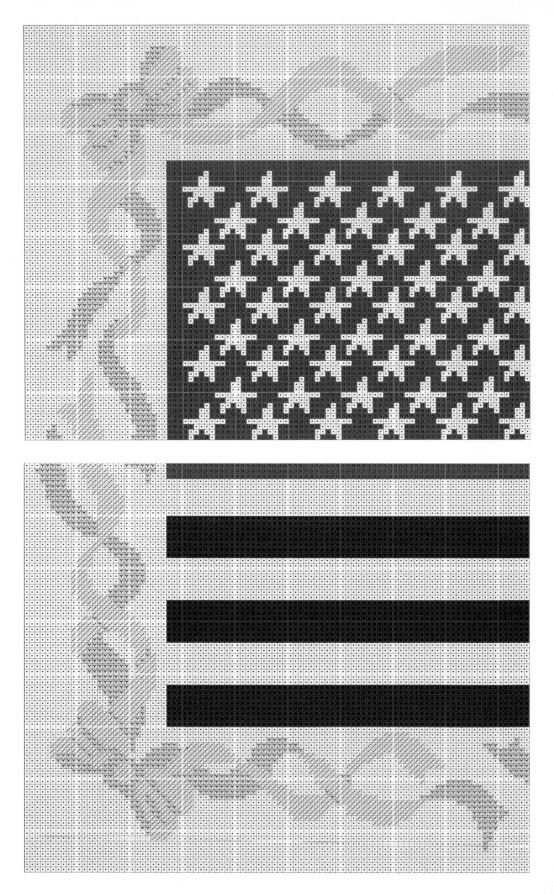

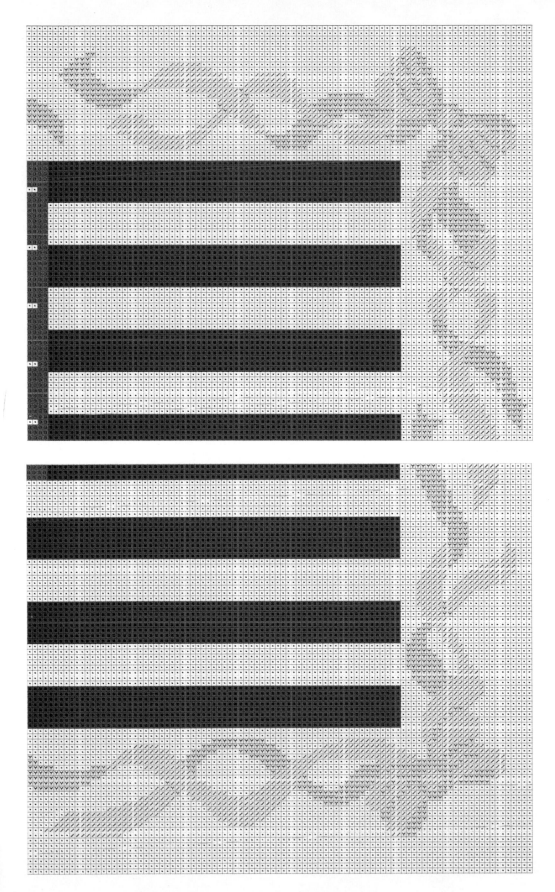

American Flag Pillow

PATERNAYAN PERSIAN WOOLS

Symbol	№	Color	Yards	Meters
Y	771	Dark Yellow	40	37
/	772	Light Yellow	80	73
B	571	Navy Blue	40	37
•	260	White (BKGD)	200	183
▓	970	Red	80	73

DESIGNER TIP

To create a jazzy touch, consider using starry or striped fabric for the pillow backing. The ribbons would look very festive stitched in pearl cotton.

AUTUMN IS ABSOLUTELY MY FAVORITE SEASON.

As kids, my sister Jill and I loved everything about Halloween, and now we enjoy "treating" the kids and decorating our porch for them. This design could be framed and hung on the front door to welcome trick-or-treaters, or after the big night, you could hang the tote bag on a wall, filled with dried bittersweet or paper lanterns.

HALLOWEEN TOTE BAG

FINISHED MEASUREMENTS

- 9½ x 9½ inches (24 x 24 cm)
- 96 stitches wide x 96 stitches high

MATERIALS

- 13 colors of Paternayan wool
- 10-mesh cotton canvas 14 x 14 inches (36 x 36 cm)
- Size 18 tapestry needle
- Finishing accessories: canvas tote bag from Bag Works (see supplier list on page 124)

WORKING THE DESIGN

Use continental stitch throughout with 3 strands of Paternayan wool in your needle.

FINISHING

I used Bag Works 13-inch (32.5 cm) orange canvas tote bag. Fold under the unstitched canvas and carefully baste it to the tote bag so that the top of the needlepoint is 1½ inches (4 cm) below the top opening of the bag and the design is centered on the front of the bag.

Halloween Tote Bag

PATERNAYAN PERSIAN WOOLS

Symbol	Nº	Color	Yards	Meters
■	221	Charcoal	5	5
⟋	203	Dark Gray	5	5
B	236	Gray	2	2
•	260	White	8	7
●	220	Black (BKGD)	65	59
✕	401	Brown	8	7
▬	822	Light Orange	15	14

Symbol	Nº	Color	Yards	Meters
Y	772	Yellow	12	11
◤	570	Dark Navy (BKGD)	20	18
8	500	Light Navy (BKGD)	45	41
✛	330	Purple	4	4
T	821	Dark Orange	8	7
G	631	Green	4	4

DESIGNER TIP

For added spookiness you can use Kreinik's Glow in the Dark fibers—white neon for the moon, ghosts, stars, and skull, and orange neon for the lettering.

I CREATED THESE BOOTIES IN HONOR OF MY COUSIN'S FIRST BABY, DONALD. *When his dad, Mark, was a child, he loved sailboats, trucks, and cars, so I used these favorites for Donald. I stitched the baby's birth date on the bottom of one bootie and his initials on the other.*

BABY BOOTIES

FINISHED MEASUREMENTS

- each sole—3¾ x 2 inches (9.5 x 5 cm); side—1 inch (2.5 cm)
- each sole: 27 stitches wide x 52 stitches high
- each top: 72 stitches wide x 62 stitches high

MATERIALS

- 7 colors of Paternayan wool
- 14-mesh cotton canvas (for both booties) 24 x 12 inches (60 x 30 cm)
- Size 22 tapestry needle
- Finishing accessories: thin red twisted cording and lining fabric

WORKING THE DESIGN

Use continental stitch throughout with 2 strands of Paternayan wool in your needle.

FINISHING

Before you stitch the bottoms of the booties using the alphabet and numbers provided, chart on graph paper the placement and spacing of the initials and letters you wish to use. After you have finished stitching the booties, cut away the excess canvas, leaving ½ inch (1.3 cm) of unstitched canvas for turning. From lightweight lining fabric, cut two tops and two sole pieces the same size as the trimmed needlepoint pieces. With right sides together, pin and then stitch together the back (heel) seams of the needlepoint tops. Then, with right sides together, pin and stitch the bootie sole to the bootie top, being careful to match front ends to front ends, and to make smoothly rounded seams along the curved front and heel of each bootie. Trim the canvas to ¼ inch (1 cm) from the seams all the way around. For both the bootie tops and soles, make perpendicular clips to the seam allowances every ¼ inch (1 cm) almost to the seam line.

Repeat these steps to make the bootie linings. Turn the needlepoint booties so the right sides face outward and turn the linings so the right sides faces inward. Insert the lining into the bootie (with wrong sides facing each other) and hand stitch them together along the top opening. As a final touch you can sew thin twisted cord along the top edge, allowing enough extra length at each end to tie into a bow at the front of the opening. To prevent the cord ends from unravelling, knot each tie end.

LEFT FOOT

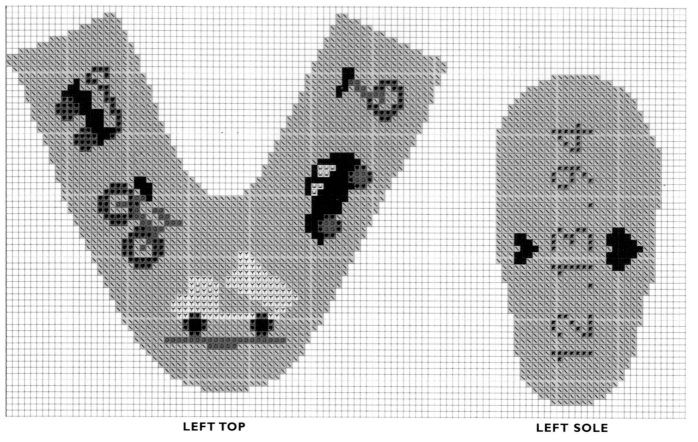

LEFT TOP   **LEFT SOLE**

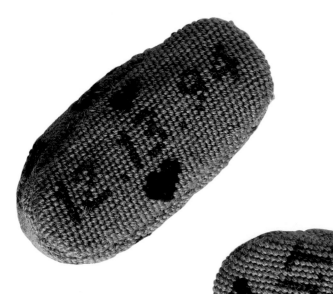

Baby Booties

PATERNAYAN PERSIAN WOOLS

Symbol	№	Color	Yard	Meters
K	611	Dark Green	5	5
▼	500	Dark Blue	4	4
G	631	Green	3	3
R	968	Red	4	4
\	545	Sky Blue (BKGD)	22	20
W	261	White	3	3
Y	703	Yellow	3	3

RIGHT FOOT

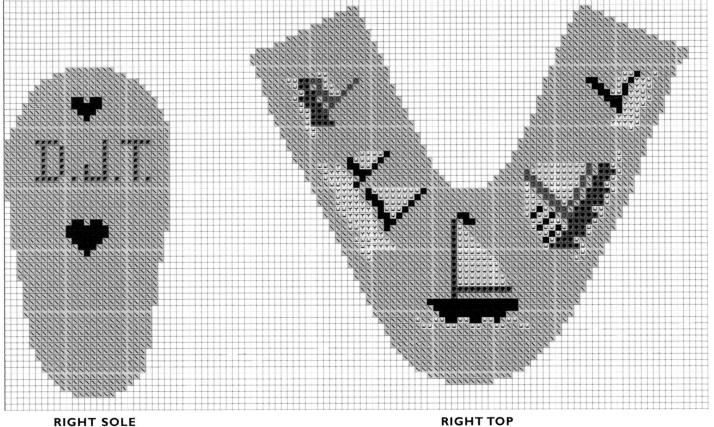

RIGHT SOLE

RIGHT TOP

ALPHABET TEMPLATE

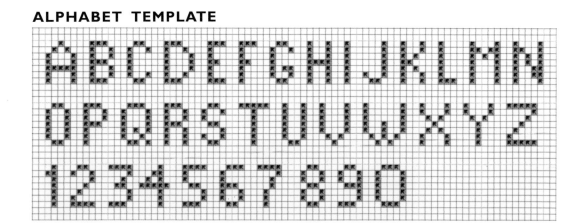

SUPPLIERS

KITS AVAILABLE FROM IN SPLENDID DETAIL LTD.

The following designs featured in this book are available as needlepoint kits: *Noah's Ark, Medieval Fox, Crazy Quilt, English Garden, Ring of Roses, Cherubs & Stars,* and *Mini-Cats.*

For ordering information please contact:
In Splendid Detail Ltd.
ATTN: Catherine Reurs
50 Marion Road
Watertown, MA 02172-4737 USA

Tel: (800) 743-0675 or (617) 926-3252
Fax: (617) 926-5883,
e-mail: crnpoint@aol.com.

Below is a listing of suppliers for the products used in my needlepoint projects. If you need help locating supplies, you can call or write to these companies for the name of the shop nearest you that carries their products. I have indicated which companies do retail mail order.

SUPPLIERS IN NORTH AMERICA

A Bear in Sheep's Clothing
ATTN: Judith Shangold
P.O. Box 770
Medford, MA 02155
Tel: (617) 438-9631   Fax: (617) 438-9631
The Teddy Bear vest (unstitched) and bears are available by mail order.

AK Designs
ATTN: Anne Karam
29350 Pacific Coast Highway #2A
Malibu, CA 90265
Tel: (310) 457-1759   Fax: (310) 457-6538
AK Designs supplied all the beads used in these projects and offers an extensive selection of beads available by mail order.

Anchor/Coats & Clark
ATTN:: Consumer Services
P.O. Box 24998
Greenville, SC 29616
Tel: (864) 234-033   Fax: (864) 281-5559
Susan Bates, a division of Coats & Clarks that manufactures Anchor embroidery floss, supplied the floss used in some projects.

Mark Arnold Cabinetmaker
423 S. Galena Road
Sunbury OH 43074
Tel: (614) 965-9618
e-mail: mnmarn@aol.comm
Mark built the footstool base for the Crazy Quilt project (page 69); it is available by mail order.

Bag Works Inc.
3301-C S. Cravens Road
Fort Worth, TX 76119
Tel: (817) 446-8080   Fax: (817) 446-8105
Bag Works' Open Tote in orange canvas (item #0100), used for the Halloween Tote Bag project (page 117), is available by mail order.

Belmont Frame & Art
ATTN: Greg Cassanos
434 Common Street
Belmont, MA 02178
Tel: (617) 489-4466
Belmont Frame & Art did all the framing for the projects in this book. The company offers fine framing of needlework using acid-free materials. This service is available by mail order.

The Caron Collection
67 Poland Street
Bridgeport, CT 06605
Tel: (203) 333-0325   Fax: (203) 333-2537
Caron Collection, manufacturer of hand-dyed threads, supplied "Watercolors" used in the Cow/Horse doorstop (page 48). For retail mail order, refer to It's a Crewel World, and the Yarn Barn of San Antonio.

Creative Furnishings
12357 Saraglen Drive
Saratoga, CA 95070
Tel: (408) 996-7745   Fax: (408) 996-0559
Creative Furnishings has a wide range of furniture for needlepoint. Call for ordering information. For the Pig Box Top (page 22), order the TBO Oblong box (8½ inches/21 cm long) in mahogany; for the base for the Pansy pincushion (page 61), order the VRP pincushion. Creative Furnishings can also supply a footstool to fit the Crazy Quilt (page 68), but it's different from the one in the photograph; order item #CR SBI to fit a 10-inch square (25 x 25 cm) needlepoint.

DMC Corporation
ATTN: Customer Service
10 Port Kearney
South Kearney, NJ 07032
Tel: (201) 589-0606   Fax: (201) 589-8931
DMC, manufacturer of DMC embroidery floss, supplied the floss and pearl cotton used in some projects.

Darice Inc.
ATTN: Customer Service
21160 Drake Road
Strongsville, OH 44136 USA
Tel: (216) 238-9150   Fax: (216) 238-1680
Darice supplied all the plastic canvas used in these projects. Available at most craft stores, look for 14-mesh clear plastic canvas (item #33275-1) and 10-mesh clear plastic canvas (item #33030-1).

Finely-Finished Needlepoint

ATTN: Marilynn Arm
9 Norwich-Salem Road
East Haddam, CT 06423
Tel: (860) 434-6296

Marilyn finished all the pillows, the Kazak checkbook cover, the Cow/Horse doorstop, and the Baby booties. She does superb finishing by mail order for clients in the USA and Canada.

Fond Memories Inc.

One Terminal Way
Norwich, CT 06360 USA
Tel: (860) 887-4789   Fax: (860) 889-7001

Fond Memories' plastic trivet covers (item #TR300) and coaster covers are available by mail order.

It's a Crewel World Inc.

231 Essex Street
Salem, MA 01970
Tel: (508) 745-9696   Fax: (508) 741-7735

It's a Crewel World is a needlework shop from which you can order any amount of a wide range of items via mail order, including The Caron Collection fibers, Paternayan Persian Wool, Zweigart canvas, DMC floss and pearl cotton, Kreinik metallics, and Rainbow Gallery fibers.

JCA Inc.

ATTN: Customer Service
35 Scales Lane
Townsend, MA 01469
Tel: (508) 597-8794   Fax: (508) 597-2632

JCA manufactures the Paternayan Persian Tapestry wool used in these projects. Call them for the name of the shop nearest you that carries Paternayan products. For retail mail order, refer to the Yarn Barn of San Antonio.

Kreinik Mfg. Co., Inc.

ATTN: Customer Service
3106 Timanus Lane, Suite #101
Baltimore, MD 21244
Tel: (410) 281-0040   Fax: (410) 281-0987

Kreinik manufactures a wide range of metallic and silk threads used in these projects. For retail mail order, refer to the Yarn Barn of San Antonio.

Madiera/Designs
by Liz Turner Diehl Inc.

P.O. Box 50355
Eugene, OR 97405
Tel: (541) 485-3381   Fax: (541) 485-7491

Designs by Liz Turner Diehl Inc. supplied the Madiera metallics used in these projects; order Madiera fibers via mail order from her.

Madiera – Division of SCS USA

9631 NE Colfax St.
Portland, OR 97220
Tel: (503) 252-1452   Fax: (503) 252-7280

SCS is the USA distributor for the Madiera metallic threads used in these projects. You can call them or write for the name of the shop nearest you that carries Madiera products.

Rainbow Gallery

7412 Fulton Avenue #5
N. Hollywood, CA 91605
Tel: (818) 982-6406   Fax: (818) 982-1476

Rainbow Gallery has a wide range of textured and metallic fibers, some of which are used in these projects. For retail mail order, refer to the Yarn Barn of San Antonio.

Sudberry House

P.O. Box 895
Old Lyme, CT 06371
Tel: (860) 739-6951   Fax: (860) 739-9267

Sudberry House supplied the Small Square tray in red (item #65646) used for the Santa Tray (page 86). For the Pig Box Top (page 22) you could substitute Sudberry Houses' Long Pen Box (item #99061), and for the Pansy Pincushion (page 61) you could substitute their Round Pincushion (item #15741).

Yarn Barn of San Antonio

4300 McCullough
San Antonio, TX 78212
Tel: (210) 826-3679   Fax: (210) 826-6722

Yarn Barn is a full-service needlework shop from which you can order any amount of a wide range of items via mail order, including Paternayan Persian Wool, Zweigart canvas, DMC floss and pearl cotton, Caron Collection fibers, Kreinik metallics, Madiera metallics, and Rainbow Gallery fibers.

Zweigart/Joan Toggitt

ATTN: Consumer Information
2 Riverview Drive
Somerset, NJ 08873
Tel: (908) 271-1949   Fax: (908) 271-0758

Zweigart supplied all the cotton needlepoint canvas used in these projects. For retail mail order, refer to the Yarn Barn of San Antonio, or Needleworkers Delight, 100 Claridge Place, Colonia, NJ 07067. Tel: (908) 388-4545.

SUPPLIERS IN UK / EUROPE

Anchor/Coats Patons Crafts

McMullen Road, Darlington
County Durham,
DL1 1YQ ENGLAND
Tel: (0325) 38 1010 Fax: (0325) 38 2300

The Caron Collection/
McCloud Craft Marketing

West Yonderton
Warlock Road, Bridge Weir
Renfrewshire, PA11 3SR SCOTLAND
Tel: (505) 612 618   Fax: (505) 612 618

DMC/DMC Creative World Ltd.
(UK only)

Pullman Road
Wigston, Leicestershire, LE18 2DY
ENGLAND
Tel: (116) 281 1040   Fax: (116) 281 3592

DMC/Dollfus Mieg & Cie (Europe)
10, Avenue Ledru-Rollin
75579 Paris Cedex 12 FRANCE
Tel: (1) 43 28 19 00   Fax: (1) 43 42 51 91

Paternayan/The Craft Collection Ltd.
Trade Dept., Terry Mills,
Westfield Road, Horbury
Wakefield, West Yorkshire, WF4
6HD ENGLAND
Tel: (01924) 810904   Fax: (01924) 810818
(for Paterna wool)

Kreinik/Monika Arnold
Zum Tauhgel, 7
D-66459 Kirkel GERMANY
Tel: (6849) 1414   Fax: (6849) 787

Madiera Garne
U.& M. Schmidt & Co. GmbH
Hans-Bunte Str. 8
Postfach 320
D-79003 Freiburg, F.R. of Germany
Tel: (0761) 510 480   Fax: (0761) 50 23 42

Sudberry House/Framecraft
372-376 Summer Lane, Hockley
Birmingham, B19 3QA ENGLAND
Tel: (1212) 212-0551   Fax: (1212) 212-0552

Zweigart and Sawitzski
ATTN: Marketing Dept.
Postfach 120
D-71043 Sindelfingen GERMANY
FAX: (70) 31 795 421

SUPPLIERS IN AUSTRALIA

Anchor/Coats Patons Crafts
89-91 Peters Avenue
Mulgrave Victoria, 3170 AUSTRALIA
Tel: (03561) 2288   Fax: (03561) 2298

The Caron Collection/Down Under Australia Pty Ltd.
559 Sydney Road
Seaforth NSW, 2092 AUSTRALIA
Tel: (2) 9948 5575   Fax: (2) 9948 7172

DMC/DMC Needlecraft Pty Ltd.
51-55 Carrington Road
Marrickville NSW, 2204 AUSTRALIA
Tel: (25) 59 30 88   Fax: (25) 59 53 38

Kreinik & Sudberry House/ Ireland Needlecraft
Unit 4, 2-4 Keppel Drive
Hallam Victoria, 3803 AUSTRALIA
Tel: (3) 9702 3222   Fax: (3) 9702 3255

Madiera/Penguin Threads Pty Ltd.
25 Izett Street
Prahan Victoria, 3181 AUSTRALIA
Tel: (3) 9529 4400   Fax: (3) 9525 1172

Paterna Wool/Stadia Handcrafts
85 Elizabeth Street
Paddington NSW, 2021 AUSTRALIA
Tel: (2) 328 7973   Fax: (2) 326 1768

Zweigart and Sawitzski
ATTN: Marketing Dept.
Postfach 120
D-71043 Sindelfingen GERMANY
FAX: 49 (70) 31 795 421

SUPPLIERS IN ASIA

Anchor/Yuki Limited
10-10-4 Kurakuen
Nishinomiya-City 662 JAPAN
Tel: (0798) 72-1563   Fax: (0798) 74-1578

DMC/Needlecraft Asia Pte Ltd.
63 Hillview Avenue #01-03
Lam Soon Industrial Bldg.
SINGAPORE 2366
Tel: 764 08 55   Fax: 764 85 50

DMC/DMC K. K.
Akazawa Building 6F
2-10-10 Kotobuki, Taito-Ku
Tokyo 111 JAPAN
Tel: 3 5828 4112   Fax: 3 5828 4117

Kreinik—Clouet Trading PTE Ltd.
21 Tagore Lane
Off Upper Thomson Road
P.O.Box 0051
SINGAPORE 2678 SG
Tel: 459 8133   Fax: 459-2867

Sudberry House & The Caron Collection—O & B Enterprises
1 Fung Shui
50 Plantation Road
The Peak, HONG KONG
Tel: (852) 284-97200   Fax: (852) 284-97369

Zweigart and Sawitzski
ATTN: Marketing Dept.
Postfach 120
D-71043 Sindelfingen GERMANY
FAX: 49 (70) 31 795 421

ACKNOWLEDGMENTS

This book is dedicated to my wonderful family. Without them it would have been impossible to create this book.

Grateful thanks to my mother, MaryAnn Parker, for her unfailing encouragement throughout my life to do what I love, and for her beautiful stitching, and for countless hours helping with everything. She is incredible!

Special thanks to my sister, Jill Reurs, whose critical eye in designing and styling doesn't miss a trick, and whose friendship, constant support, and help with and belief in my work really mean everything.

Thanks to my husband, Jiri Stanislav, for his love and for encouraging me to create books despite the fact that he has to put up with my mini-offices spreading all over the house, and the general chaos that producing a book creates. His sense of humor pulled us all through the process.

A particular thank you to Jon Wallen for his superb photography.

Many thanks to all the talented people at Lark Books for their enthusiasm and support. Very special thanks to Rob Pulleyn for making this book happen, and to my editor, Deborah Morgenthal, for her friendship, elegant editing, and sense of humor. Deep appreciation to Chris Bryant for his beautiful, open-minded (!) styling and for making the book look so good.

Grateful thanks to Jan and Simon Braun for generously allowing us to use their beautiful house for the location shots. Special thanks to Brian Hasmuk of Antiques on Broadway in Asheville, North Carolina, and Judith Shangold of A Bear in Sheep's Clothing for kindly loaning us wonderful props. Thanks also to New Morning Gallery in Asheville, North Carolina, for loaning us the wooden Noah's Ark on page 19, made by Gunther Keil of Wild Apples. Thanks to Barbara Bangser for doing some of the charts. Thanks also to Luck McElreath for making the gorgeous fresh flower garland on page 53.

Particular thanks to the following companies that generously provided the following products. For fibers: Anchor/Susan Bates Inc., Lois Caron of The Caron Collection, MaryAnn Blackburn of DMC Corp., Liz Turner Diehl of Designs by Liz Turner Diehl, Alan Getz of JCA Inc., Doug and Jacqueline Kreinik of Kreinik Manufacturing Co. Inc., and John Schatteles of Rainbow Gallery. For needlepoint furnishings and other supplies: Anne Karam of AK Designs, Mark Arnold Cabinetry, Carolyn Guthrie of Bag Works Inc., Greg Cassanos of Belmont Art & Frame, Elaine Clabeaux of Creative Furnishings, Marilynn Arm of Finely Finished Needlepoint, Judith Beers of Sudberry House, and Rudy Heukels of Zweigart/Joan Toggitt Ltd.

INDEX